SMOOTHIE DIET

Easy Smoothies Recipes for Weight Loss and Good Health

(Delicious Smoothie Cookbook Recipes for Rapid Weight Loss)

Arturo Beaver

Published by Sharon Lohan

© **Arturo Beaver**

All Rights Reserved

Smoothie Diet: Easy Smoothies Recipes for Weight Loss and Good Health (Delicious Smoothie Cookbook Recipes for Rapid Weight Loss)

ISBN 978-1-990334-41-2

All rights reserved. No part of this guide may be reproduced in any form without permission in writing from the publisher except in the case of brief quotations embodied in critical articles or reviews.

Legal & Disclaimer

The information contained in this book is not designed to replace or take the place of any form of medicine or professional medical advice. The information in this book has been provided for educational and entertainment purposes only.

The information contained in this book has been compiled from sources deemed reliable, and it is accurate to the best of the Author's knowledge; however, the Author cannot guarantee its accuracy and validity and cannot be held liable for any errors or omissions. Changes are periodically made to this book. You must consult your doctor or get professional medical advice before using any of the suggested remedies, techniques, or information in this book.

Table of contents

Part 1 1
Introduction: Vegan FAQs 2
"You're vegan? What do you even eat?" 2
"Where do you get your protein?" 2
"Can you eat this?" 6
"Is this really vegan?" 6
"Is being vegan expensive?" 8
"Is being vegan a lot of work?" 10
Smoothie Tips 11
About Sweeteners 13
Simple Smoothies 16
Granola Smoothie 16
Ginger Berry 18
Pink Princess 20
Banana Nut 22
Chocolate Kickstart 24
Peach Carrot 26
Banana Oatmeal 28
Sneaky Smoothie 30
Superfood Smoothies 32
Glowing Skin 32
Rainbow Smoothie 34
Chai Tea Smoothie 37
Orange Power 39
Under the Weather Smoothie 41

Allergy Season	43
Daily Detox	45
Chocolate Protein	47
Nuts & Dates	49
Ayurvedic Smoothie	51
Fig Shake	53
Winter Blues	55
Green Smoothies	57
Pineapple-Mint	57
Tummy Tamer	59
Tropical Greens	61
Herbal Remedy	63
Strawberry Basil	65
Ginger Lime	66
Creamy Greens	68
Green Tart	70
Morning Matcha	72
Smoothie Bowls	74
Sunrise Smoothie Bowl	74
Chocolate Mint Bowl	76
Banana Split Bowl	78
Nutella Bowl	80
Ipanema Bowl	82
Beauty Bowl	84
Ocean Breeze	86
Strawberry Oatmeal	88
Turbo Greens Protein	90

Dragon Fruit Bowl	92
Key Lime Pie Smoothie Bowl	94
Dessert Smoothies	96
Cinnamon Roll	96
Peaches and Cream	98
Autumn Delight	100
Piña Colada	102
Strawberry Rosewater	104
Gingerbread Smoothie	106
Pumpkin Pie Jar	108
Hot Chocolate	110
Chocolate Cherry	112
Carrot Cake	114
Part 2	116
Introduction	117
Chapter 1: Losing Weight	120
Plan the weight loss	120
Balanced diet	121
Exercise/yoga	121
Foods that assists natural weight loss	121
Chapter 2: All You Need to Know About Detox	123
What is detox?	123
Foods that assist in cleansing and detoxifying your body	123
Chapter 3: Food and Nutrition	126
Natural Methods for Weight loss and Detoxification	127
Food to avoid while losing weight and detoxification	129
Chapter 4: Smoothies and Their Benefits	131

Why smoothies?	131
Chapter 5: Nutrient-packed smoothie recipes	132
Smoothies for slimming down	133
The green punch	133
Soy Smoothie	134
Cinnamon apple punch	136
Asparagus smoothie	137
Banana with berries punch	138
Green spinach smoothie	139
Low calorie vitality smoothie	140
Cherry berry smoothie	142
Green veggie smoothie	143
Fruit cracker smoothie	144
Carrot pepperonia smoothie	145
Coconut cucumber smoothie	146
Ginger spin smoothie	147
Avocado lime smoothie	148
Pacific Smoothie	149
Penny's Smoothie	149
Banana strawberry Smoothie	150
Fig Smoothie	151
Orange Smoothie	151
All Around Good Smoothie	152
Pumpkin Smoothie	153
Razzy Blue Smoothie	154
Refreshing Smoothie	154
Key lime pie smoothie	155

Afternoon Smoothie	156
Rosy Ginger peach Smoothie	156
Watermelon Smoothie	157
Black and Blueberry Smoothie	158
Tasty Strawberries Smoothie	158
Coconut Banango Smoothie	159
Amaretto Smoothie	160
BFF Smoothie	160
Cinnapear Smoothie	161
Tofuberry smoothie	162
Gator Smoothie	162
Sour Smoothie	163
Milk and banana smoothie	163
All-fruit Smoothie	164
Fruit and yogurt smoothie	164
Raspberry Banana Smoothie	165
Mango peach and banana smoothie	166
Tropical Smoothie with kale smoothie	166
Pineapple and banana smoothie	167
Green power and Mojito Smoothie	168
Super Smooth	168
Island Smoothie	169
Hailey's Smoothie	170
Avocado Smoothie	170
Yummy Smoothie	171
Peach Smoothie	171
B and L Strawberry Smooth	172

- Mango peach Smoothie 173
- Coconut Berry Green Smoothies 173
- Banana Mango Green Smoothie 174
- Orange Avocado Green Smoothie 174
- Banana Nut Green Smoothie 175
- Cherry Wheatgrass Green Smoothie 176
- Banana Rice Protein Green Smoothie 176
- Berry Protein Green Smoothie 177
- Cucumber Strawberry Green Smoothie 178
- Cranberry Green Smoothie 179
- Carrot Apple Green Smoothie 179
- Green Berry Smoothie 180
- Apple Pear Green Smoothie 181
- Banana Pear Green Smoothie 182
- Orange Spinach Green Smoothie 182
- Papaya Lemon Green Smoothie 183
- Mango Banana Green Smoothie 184
- Banana Nut Green Smoothie 184
- Watermelon Ginger Green Smoothie 185
- Berry Coconut Green Smoothie 185
- Conclusion 187

Part 1

Introduction: Vegan FAQs

"You're vegan? What do you even eat?"

You've probably heard this question 101 times since you decided to make the ethical and sustainable choice to go vegan. Your answer is probably, "Umm… everything that doesn't come from animals?" People are usually flabbergasted by this, but the fact is that a lot of food is already vegan—and with a little creativity and the right ingredients, you can vegan-ify almost anything else.

People often think that being vegan is limiting or a diet, but that's just not the case. Most vegans love food; they just choose to make their ethics and values a priority when choosing what to eat.

If you're new to vegan cooking, you might have some questions, so before you jump into the delicious and easy recipes in this book, take some time to read the introduction for tips, tricks, and helpful information.

"Where do you get your protein?"

This is another annoying question that vegans get asked all of the time. People act like meat and dairy are the only sources of protein in the world!

The fact is that most people in developed countries actually get too much protein. If you're new to the vegan diet, you should spend some time counting protein and planning your meals to make sure you're getting enough, but rest assured that protein deficiency is relatively rare.

Amino acids are organic compounds responsible for a wide variety of processes in the body. When they bind together in long chains, they make proteins. While our bodies can produce many of their own amino acids, there are nine types which the human body cannot create on its own. This means that we rely on our food for these.

Something vegans should keep in mind is that not all sources of protein have all of the amino acids that you need. In fact, most don't. But no need to worry: As long as you are able to get all of these amino acids within one day, you should be fine.

Practically, that means that you can't rely on just one or two sources of protein a day. When you're eating vegan, a good rule of thumb is that each meal should have two kinds of protein. This may sound like trouble, but you'd be surprised how many foods contain protein. Once you get used to eating a vegan diet and creative cooking, getting enough protein is something you won't even think about.

Check with a nutritionist or online to find out how many grams of protein you should be eating in a day. To make things easier, each of the recipes in this cookbook details how many grams of protein are in a serving.

If you're sick of answering the protein question, check out these common vegan proteins, how to use them, and their nutritional benefits.

Black Beans

Did you know that the darker the color of a bean, the more antioxidants it has? Black beans are definitely a vegan staple. With 15 grams of protein per cooked cup, plus 15 grams of fiber, black beans are a great way to make a meal more filling. From Mexican food to brownies (that's right, brownies) this cookbook has plenty of recipes that integrate this filling bean.

Walnuts

Nuts and seeds are another source of protein for vegans. Rich in healthy fats and protein, this nut is a great snack or addition to a meal to help you feel full. Add crushed walnuts to desserts, pasta, or even pizza!

Quinoa

Quinoa might just be the king of vegan protein. Once eaten by Incan warriors, this seed (yes, quinoa is technically a seed, although it's served as a grain) serves up a complete amino acid group. That means that if you eat quinoa, you won't have to worry about combining proteins. Quinoa is great in salads, made into a veggie burger, or served with curry. You can even find pasta made out of quinoa at your local health food store.

Chickpeas

This versatile legume isn't just for hummus (although hummus is a delicious vegan staple you should master). Chickpeas have 14.5 grams of protein per cooked cup, plus 11 grams of fiber, manganese, and folate, a nutrient important for women. Chickpeas are great in curries, salads, stews, and so much more.

Oats

There's no vegan breakfast quite as delicious as oatmeal loaded with cinnamon and brown sugar, and that's hardly the only good thing about oats. Oats have been proven to help reduce cholesterol, so if you went vegan for your heart health (good move) you should add oats into your diet whenever you can. Gluten-free? No worries! You can easily find gluten-free oats and oat flour.

Tofu

Made from soy beans, tofu is a vegan classic, but most non-vegans turn their nose up at it. Why has tofu gotten such a bad reputation? Who knows, but with the recipes in this book, even your carnivorous friends will become tofu enthusiasts. With just 178 calories—but 12 grams of protein—per serving, no vegan diet is complete without tofu. Bread it, fry it, bake it, or blend it; the possibilities are endless, so get creative with this protein-packed treat.

Be sure to buy GMO-free tofu, as the health effects of consuming genetically modified soybeans are unclear.

Lentils

Lentils are a legume that appears across the world, from French cuisine to Indian food, and frequently in this cookbook. With 18 grams of protein per cooked cup, lentils are a perfect addition to stews, veggie burgers, salads, and meat replacements.

"Can you eat this?"

The quick answer to this question is yes. As a vegan, you can technically eat anything; you just choose not to. Whether you chose to become vegan for health reasons, weight loss, the environment, your love of animals, or all of the above, don't let your lifestyle choice make you feel limited. With some practice and creativity, eating vegan can open new doors of culinary delights, rather than closing them.

"Is this really vegan?"

You may find yourself asking that when you're eating at a vegan restaurant. How can they make food so creamy, buttery, or cheesy without using dairy? The answer is vegan hacks. There are a few staples that every vegan should be familiar with. These staples help to emulate flavors not usually associated with a plant-based diet.

Once you've mastered these ingredients, you'll hear a chorus of "Is this really vegan?" at your next dinner party.

Cashews

No vegan pantry is complete without cashews. Soak these babies in water for a few hours, drain, and blend with herbs and spices to make creamy dipping sauces, or with sugar and cocoa powder for vegan ice cream.

The high-protein possibilities are practically endless. Cashew "milk" shakes, anyone?

Nutritional Yeast

Nutritional yeast has a cheesy flavor, making it most vegans' first choice when it comes to cheese replacements. It's super-low in calories but high in protein, with just 40 calories and 3 grams of protein per tablespoon. Most vegans just can't live without nutritional yeast, and retailers know this; that's why it often comes fortified with vitamins that vegans tend to lack, like vitamin B_{12}. Why take a multivitamin if you can just eat creamy, delicious vegan queso every day?

Tahini

Like cashews and nutritional yeast, tahini is an easy way to add more protein to a meal. It's also rich in healthy fats. Tahini can bring creaminess to a recipe, as well as a nutty flavor, making it a great addition to curries and stir fries. Tahini is also a perfect base for making salad dressings and glazes. If you have a nut allergy, you can use tahini in place of nuts in lots of recipes.

Avocado

Avocado is another way to enhance creaminess in recipes. With 13 grams of fiber and 4 grams of protein per serving, avocado is as healthy as it is tasty. Use avocado to make a killer chocolate mousse or an indulgent pasta sauce. Add an avocado to a smoothie to make it even creamier.

Flax Seeds

Flax seeds are an easy way to add protein to any meal. Flax seeds are also high in omega fatty acids, which are super-important for radiant skin. Just throw some ground flax seeds into a smoothie for an instant boost. Doctors also recommend adding omega fatty acids to your diet during the winter in conjunction with vitamin D to fight off the winter blues.

As if that weren't enough, these little seeds are also a great egg replacement. Mix a tablespoon of ground flax seeds with a tablespoon of water for an instant egg substitute that you can use in almost any recipe.

Make sure you buy ground flax seeds, because your body is unable to digest them whole.

Cauliflower

Cauliflower is a low-carbohydrate replacement for rice, potatoes, and sometimes even flour, making this one of the world's most versatile vegetables. Low in calories, but high in vitamin C, cauliflower is a nutritional win-win. When cooked and blended, cauliflower gets super creamy, making it a perfect nutrient-dense cream replacement. Add to soups and curries in place of heavy cream, or use it to make "cheese."

"Is being vegan expensive?"

Some specialty items might be more expensive, but a vegan diet does not have to be an expensive endeavor.

When you go to the grocery store, what's usually more expensive, meat or vegetables?

The best way to save money on a vegan diet is by shopping at local farmers' markets and buying the produce that is in season. Buying from local farmers not only supports your community, it's also more eco-friendly because the produce does not have to be transported long distances.

Check out this guide to seasonal produce.

Fall
Pomegranate, butternut squash, apples, pears, figs, sweet potatoes, arugula, beets, peppers, broccoli, celery, eggplant, cranberries, potatoes, lettuce, mushrooms, limes, pumpkins, green beans, zucchini.

Winter
Beets, cabbage, oranges, Brussels sprouts, onions, clementines, kale, cauliflower, leeks, grapefruit, lemons, mandarin oranges, shallots, radishes, turnips, winter squash, tangerines.

Spring
Asparagus, strawberries, cherries, rhubarb, kumquats, fava beans, apricots, chard, kiwis, new potatoes, peas, spinach, spring onions.

Summer
Basil, avocados, peaches, cantaloupes, blackberries, mangoes, bell peppers, lemongrass, chard, blueberries, okra, chickpeas, melons, collard greens, grapes,

cucumbers, figs, plums, raspberries, spinach, watermelons, summer squash, nectarines.

Organic produce is often more expensive than conventional, but it is better for the environment and your body because it does not contain harmful pesticides and other chemicals. That being said, it's not always necessary to eat only organic produce.

Experts have developed lists called the Clean 15 and the Dirty Dozen. The Clean 15 are the 15 fruits and veggies that have the lowest levels of pesticides and are therefore safe to eat even if they aren't organic. The Dirty Dozen are the 12 fruits and vegetables highest in chemicals. You shouldn't eat these unless you can get them organic.

The Clean 15
Corn, pineapple, cauliflower, honeydew, avocado, kiwi, onions, eggplant, cabbage, sweet peas, asparagus, papaya, mangos, cantaloupe, grapefruit.

The Dirty Dozen
Spinach, pears, strawberries, bell peppers, celery, nectarines, potatoes, cherries, apples, grapes, peaches, tomatoes.

"Is being vegan a lot of work?"

Being vegan is about as much work as you want it to be. Plenty of vegans consider their diet not just a lifestyle choice but also a hobby. Cooking vegan is fun and requires creativity, so when you see your vegan friends cooking for hours every day, it's probably because they love cooking and eating delicious, healthy meals, not because they have to.

Being a vegan can be easy and low maintenance. Plenty of the recipes in this cookbook don't even require cooking and can be made in 10 minutes or less.

With all of these delicious yet nutritious options, being a vegan is really fun. As an added bonus, vegan food is usually lower in calories, which means you get to eat seemingly decadent meals without harming your health or waistline.

When vegan food can be this healthy, but taste oh so good, why would you ever eat meat or dairy?

Smoothie Tips

Smoothies are a great way to add a powerful punch of nutrition to your day with practically no work in the kitchen. Check out these tips if you're looking to add smoothies to your daily life or detox regimen.

Replace Coffee
It's no secret that drinking a lot of caffeine in the morning can make you jittery all day. It also makes you crash in the afternoon, creating an endless cycle of caffeine addiction. Coffee may instantly perk you up, but drinking too much has an acidic effect on the body and wreaks havoc on your digestive system.

The answer? Replace your morning coffee with a healthy, nutrient-dense smoothie. A green smoothie with protein in the morning is guaranteed to jump-start your digestive system and metabolism and give you sustained energy for hours.

Think Outside the Box

Think smoothies are just for fruit? Think again! Herbs, tea, spices, nut butters, seeds, veggies and greens all make great additions to smoothies. Next time you have veggies in the fridge about to go bad, just throw them into your morning smoothie!

Smoothies are more than just breakfast, though. A well-thought-out smoothie with protein can make for an easy meal any time you don't have time to cook. They're also a great option as an afternoon snack for the kids.

On a diet, but still love dessert? Vegan smoothies are your answer. This cookbook features a whole section of dessert smoothies and another on smoothie bowls. With all of these options, there's no need to deny your sweet tooth!

Meal Prep

Meal prepping can change your life. If you think you don't have time to make healthy meals, meal prepping is the answer. At the beginning of the week, plan the smoothies you want to make. Put all of the ingredients, already cut and measured, into a Ziploc bag or Mason jar (more sustainable). That way, whenever you want a healthy meal or snack, you just dump the entire contents into the blender and serve.

Embrace Your Freezer

Freezing fruits and veggies that are nearing their expiration date is a great way to save money and avoid waste, and they also make great additions to smoothies. Use a cup of frozen berries in place of ice in a recipe for some extra fiber and antioxidants.

Frozen bananas are especially useful because they not only deliver potassium and fiber but can also serve as a great base for a thick and creamy smoothie bowl. Frozen bananas can totally amp up your smoothie game, and the overripe ones are just perfect for this. Next time you're at the farmers' market, ask if you can buy some of the overripe bananas at a discount. Don't be afraid of brown spots! Adding banana to a smoothie often means that you don't need to add sweetener.

Taste First

None of the recipes in this cookbook call for refined sugar or artificial flavors, but even natural sweeteners can be high in sugar and calories. Before you sweeten your smoothie, it's a good idea to taste it first—you may find it's perfect just the way it is.

About Sweeteners

Some people like very sweet smoothies, while others prefer something milder, so feel free to adjust the sweetness level of all of the smoothies in this cookbook. If you like sweet smoothies, check out these vegan sweeteners sourced from nature. There's no need to add super-addictive refined sugar to any of these recipes.

Maple Syrup

All-natural maple syrup is one of Mother Nature's best gifts. Its pleasing sweetness is complemented by a subtle earth flavor. Maple syrup is great in any recipe, but goes especially well with dessert smoothies. Maple syrup pairs nicely with warm spices like cinnamon, ginger, and chai tea. It also goes great with fall flavors like butternut squash or pumpkin. Unlike sugar, maple syrup is high in antioxidants and helps to reduce inflammation. While those with irritable bowel syndrome usually have to avoid honey, 100% vegan maple syrup is safe for them to eat. When shopping for maple syrup, be sure to read the ingredients list, because some "maple syrups" in the grocery store may be made in part or entirely of corn syrup and artificial flavors!

Dates

These Middle Eastern delights are one of the healthiest sweeteners and make a great addition to any smoothie. Add one or more depending on how sweet you'd like your smoothie, but be sure to pit your dates before you add them to the blender. Dates are also a natural energy booster, so eat them in the morning or before a workout!

Fruit Juice

All-natural fruit juice can add the sweetness you need to a smoothie while also providing the liquid that makes it easier to blend. Just make sure your fruit juice doesn't have any added sugar. Opt for juices like orange or apple if you're on a budget. If not, pomegranate or acai juice can add much-needed antioxidants and some unique flavor. Coconut water is another great option for something more tropical!

Bananas
Bananas make for a sweetener filled with fiber and much-needed minerals and vitamins. Bananas are loaded with magnesium, so add one after a workout or when you're on your period

Blackstrap Molasses
Molasses is an antioxidant-dense, low-glycemic sweetener. Molasses is especially high in iron, a nutrient that vegans often lack, so menstruating or pregnant women should consider integrating this sweetener into their meals.

Simple Smoothies

Granola Smoothie

This granola smoothie is a great option for breakfast. Granola adds flavorful crunch along with cholesterol-lowering fiber, while butternut squash is loaded with vitamin A and nut butter adds heart-healthy fat and protein.

Yields: 2 – Prep. Time: 5 min. – Cooking Time: 0 min.

Ingredients
1 apple
1 pear
½ cup vegan milk, vanilla
¼ cup roasted butternut squash
1 tablespoon nut butter
¼ cup granola, cinnamon flavored
1 tablespoon maple syrup (if desired)
Ice

Preparation
1. Combine all ingredients except the granola and blend until smooth. Slowly add milk as needed.
2. When the smoothie is blended to your desired consistency, add granola and pulse for a few seconds. You just want to mix it in a little.

Nutrition facts per serving:
Calories 246, total fat 7 g, carbs 44 g,
Protein 7 g, sodium 48 mg

Ginger Berry

This smoothie is so simple, but it's loaded with nutrients. Mixed berries bring to the table fiber, antioxidants, and vitamin C, while fresh ginger is a great anti-inflammatory. Ground flaxseed adds healthy fats that make your skin glow! This smoothie is perfect if you feel like you're getting sick. If your mixed berries aren't frozen, that's OK: just add some ice instead.

Yields: 2 – Prep. Time: 5 min. – Cooking Time: 0 min.

Ingredients
1 cup mixed berries, frozen
1 tablespoon fresh ginger, grated
½ cup apple juice
1 tablespoon flaxseeds

Preparation

1. Combine all ingredients and blend until smooth. Slowly add juice as needed.

Nutrition facts per serving:
Calories 92, total fat 2 g, carbs 19 g,
Protein 1 g, sodium 4 mg

Pink Princess

The beautiful pink color of this smoothie is a great way to convince your picky princess to eat her daily fruit and veggie servings. Beets deliver a bright pink color plus sweetness, not to mention fiber, antioxidants, and vitamin C. This is also a great smoothie for pregnant women, because beets have much-needed folate. Topped with vegan whipped cream, this is a delightful treat.

Yields: 4 – Prep. Time: 5 min. – Cooking Time: 0 min.

Ingredients
1 red apple, Honeycrisp recommended
1 cup strawberries
½ cup raspberries
½ cup beets, cooked
1 banana
½ cup water (or as needed)
Vegan whipped cream

Ice

Preparation
1. Combine all ingredients and blend until smooth. Slowly add water and ice as needed.
2. Top with whipped cream and serve.

Nutrition facts per serving:
Calories 126, total fat 4 g, carbs 24 g,
Protein 2 g, sodium 123 mg

Banana Nut

This smoothie tastes like banana bread, but with less carbs. It can even be made as a gluten-free alternative to banana bread. Nuts and flaxseed serve up protein and healthy fats that will keep you feeling satiated for hours. Bananas provide fiber and potassium for a heart-healthy treat.

Yields: 2 – Prep. Time: 5 min. – Cooking Time: 0 min.

Ingredients
2 bananas
¼ cup granola
1 cup vegan milk, vanilla
¼ cup chopped nuts of choice, unsalted (plus more for topping)
1 tablespoon flaxseed
Vegan whipped cream
Cinnamon (to taste)

Ice

Preparation
1. Combine all ingredients, except for the granola, and blend until smooth. Slowly add ice and milk as needed.
2. When the smoothie is blended to your desired consistency, add granola and pulse for a few seconds. You just want to mix it in a little.
3. Top with whipped cream, crushed nuts, and cinnamon

Nutrition facts per serving:
Calories 366, total fat 20 g, carbs 45 g,
Protein 9 g, sodium 31 mg

Chocolate Kickstart

Drinking multiple cups of coffee every day is bad for your mood and digestive system, but that doesn't mean you have to cut coffee out entirely. This smoothie is a great option whether you're trying to wean yourself off of coffee or you just love mocha flavors. Plus, raw cocoa powder is ridiculously high in antioxidants.

Yields: 2 – Prep. Time: 5 min. – Cooking Time: 0 min.

Ingredients
1 banana, frozen
½ cup vegan milk
½ cup coffee, cold
1 tablespoon flaxseed
1 tablespoon nut butter (optional)

2 tablespoons cocoa powder (or chocolate protein powder)
1 tablespoon maple syrup

Preparation
1. Combine all ingredients and blend until smooth. Slowly add milk as needed.

Nutrition facts per serving:
Calories 178, total fat 8 g, carbs 27 g,
Protein 5 g, sodium 27 mg

Peach Carrot

This smoothie is a bright idea when you're looking for something to use all of those summer peaches for! Carrots are high in vitamin A, very important for your skin and eyesight, while sweet peaches are loaded with antioxidants and vitamin C, making this easy smoothie a nutritional powerhouse.

Yields: 2 – Prep. Time: 5 min. – Cooking Time: 0 min.

Ingredients
½ cup shredded carrots
2 peaches, pitted
1 mango
1 cup apple juice or water
Ice

Preparation
1. Combine all ingredients and blend until smooth. Slowly add liquid as needed.

Nutrition facts per serving:
Calories 189, total fat 1 g, carbs 46 g,
Protein 2 g, sodium 49 mg

Banana Oatmeal

Between fiber-filled oatmeal and banana, this smoothie couldn't be healthier for your heart. This smoothie actually has 12 grams of fiber per serving, which is more than a third of the fiber you need in a day! Plus, vegan yogurt delivers much-needed probiotics, making this smoothie a great choice for gut health too.

Yields: 2 – Prep. Time: 5 min. – Cooking Time: 0 min.

Ingredients
1 banana
½ cup vegan yogurt (coconut or soy)
½ cup vegan milk, vanilla
¼ cup rolled oats
1 tablespoon flaxseed
1 date, pitted
Ice

Preparation
1. Combine all ingredients and blend until smooth. Slowly add ice as needed.

Nutrition facts per serving:
Calories 230, total fat 5 g, carbs 42 g,
Protein 7 g, sodium 40 mg

Sneaky Smoothie

This smoothie is perfect for tricking kids into eating their veggies. Sweet berries, high in antioxidants, cover up the taste of matchstick carrots, which deliver vitamin A and fiber.

Yields: 4 – Prep. Time: 5 min. – Cooking Time: 0 min.

Ingredients
1 cup strawberries
½ cup mixed berries
½ cup (or to taste) matchstick or shredded carrots
1 cup vegan milk, unsweetened
1 banana
Ice

Preparation
1. Combine all ingredients and blend until smooth. Slowly add ice as needed.

Nutrition facts per serving:
Calories 80, total fat 1 g, carbs 16 g,

Protein 3 g, sodium 45 mg

Superfood Smoothies

Glowing Skin

One of the best things you can do to get glowing skin is eating a high fiber diet, because fiber helps your body remove toxins that lead to acne. Papaya is one of the best individual foods for your skin because it is rich in antioxidants, vitamin A, and an enzyme called papain. Papain is a coveted enzyme often seen in face products, and it also improves your digestion. Pineapple is another great treat for your skin. It contains an anti-inflammatory enzyme called bromelain, so add pineapple to your diet if you're struggling with redness or cystic acne.

Yields: 4 – Prep. Time: 5 min. – Cooking Time: 0 min.

Ingredients
1 apple
½ cup pineapple
½ cup papaya
½ cup strawberry
¼ cup pomegranate seeds
¼ cup beets, peeled and cooked
1 cup orange juice
1 tablespoon flaxseed
Ice

Preparation
1. Combine all ingredients and blend until smooth. Slowly add ice and orange juice as needed.

Nutrition facts per serving:
Calories 109, total fat 1 g, carbs 24 g,
Protein 2 g, sodium 63 mg

Rainbow Smoothie

This smoothie is so beautiful that it's yet another way to coax kids into eating their fruits and veggies. Serve in a large Mason jar so you can see all of the colors. This smoothie may call for a lot of ingredients and a little more effort, but the results are picture perfect. Plus, with chia seeds, turmeric, and spirulina, it's crazy healthy. Spirulina in particular is a superfood that helps to detoxify the body. It has even been shown to help patients suffering from HIV and cancer.

Yields: 4 – Prep. Time: 5 min. – Cooking Time: 0 min.

Ingredients
Red
¼ cup strawberries
¼ cup raspberries
1 apple
½ tablespoon maple syrup
½ tablespoon chia seeds

Coconut water (as needed)
Ice
Orange
1 peach
½ mango
¼ cup sweet potato
¼ teaspoon turmeric
Orange juice (as needed)
Ice
Green
½ cup spinach
1 kiwi
1 green apple
¼ cup pineapple
½ tablespoon maple syrup
Coconut water (as needed)
Ice
Blue
½ cup blueberries
½ cup blackberries
1 banana
1 teaspoon blue spirulina powder
½ tablespoon maple syrup
Coconut water (as needed)
Ice

Preparation
1. Combine ingredients for one color in the blender. Blend, slowly adding ice and liquid as needed. Pour into glasses, then clean the blender out between

colors. Repeat until you've worked your way through all of the colors.
2. Makes 4 large servings.

Nutrition facts per serving:
Calories 210, total fat 1 g, carbs 50 g, Protein 3 g, sodium 49 mg

Chai Tea Smoothie

Chai tea is filled with warming spices like cinnamon, ginger, and cardamom that are amazing for your digestive system. It has caffeine, too, so this smoothie can even be a great replacement for coffee in the morning!

Yields: 2 – Prep. Time: 5 min. – Cooking Time: 0 min.

Ingredients
¾ cup brewed chai tea
1 banana, frozen
½ cup coconut milk (or as needed)
2 tablespoons maple syrup
½ teaspoon vanilla extract

Preparation
1. Combine all ingredients and blend until smooth. Slowly add coconut milk as needed.

Nutrition facts per serving:

Calories 256, total fat 13 g, carbs 36 g, Protein 3 g, sodium 31 mg

Orange Power

This smoothie is jam-packed with vitamin A, which is great for preventing age-related eye conditions and also works wonders for your skin. Bright yellow turmeric may just be one of the most powerful spices; as a supercharged anti-inflammatory, turmeric is believed to help prevent cancer and Alzheimer's.

Yields: 2 – Prep. Time: 5 min. – Cooking Time: 0 min.

Ingredients
1 mango
1 peach
¼ cup shredded carrots
¼ cup sweet potato, peeled and cooked
1 cup orange juice
½ teaspoon turmeric
1 tablespoon maple syrup or 1 date, pitted
Ice

Preparation

1. Combine all ingredients and blend until smooth. Slowly add orange juice as needed.

Nutrition facts per serving:
Calories 264, total fat 1 g, carbs 64 g,
Protein 4 g, sodium 117 mg

Under the Weather Smoothie

When you feel like you're getting sick, don't rush to the doctor to get costly antibiotics. Nature has plenty of antibiotics of its own! This smoothie is filled with all-natural antibiotics, like fresh ginger, and loaded with vitamin C, so don't skip this recipe come cold and flu season.

Yields: 2 – Prep. Time: 5 min. – Cooking Time: 0 min.

Ingredients
1 banana
1 tablespoon ginger, fresh
½ cup vegan yogurt
½ cup orange juice
1 cup mixed berries
½ lime, juiced
½ cup leafy greens
1 tablespoon chia seeds
1 date, pitted

Preparation
1. Combine all ingredients and blend until smooth. Slowly add orange juice as needed.

Nutrition facts per serving:
Calories 264, total fat 1 g, carbs 64 g,
Protein 4 g, sodium 117 mg

Allergy Season

Reducing allergy symptoms is all about eating natural antihistamines and anti-inflammatory foods like ginger, lemon, and green tea. Mint also serves as a natural antihistamine while thinning mucus in the body.

Yields: 2 – Prep. Time: 5 min. – Cooking Time: 0 min.

Ingredients
1 cup mixed berries
1 apple
1 cup green tea
1 lemon, juiced
¼ cup pomegranate seeds
¼ cup mint leaves
¼ cup kale
1 tablespoon ginger, fresh
1 tablespoon flaxseed
2 dates, pitted
Ice

Preparation
1. Combine all ingredients and blend until smooth. Slowly add green tea as needed.

Nutrition facts per serving:
Calories 165, total fat 2 g, carbs 39 g,
Protein 2 g, sodium 7 mg

Daily Detox

Each day we consume tons of toxins, from pollution in the air to chemicals in our beauty products to pesticides in our food. You may think that a detox is something you do every once in a while, but there are plenty of foods that can help you detox every day. Foods rich in fiber and antioxidants can help you avoid the rapid aging and immune system damage that comes from consuming too many toxins.

Yields: 2 – Prep. Time: 5 min. – Cooking Time: 0 min.

Ingredients
1 lemon, juiced
1 apple
1 cup pineapple
¼ cup beets, cooked and peeled
½ cup green tea
1 tablespoon ginger

1 tablespoon flaxseed
1 tablespoon maple syrup (if desired)
Ice

Preparation
1. Combine all ingredients and blend until smooth. Slowly add green tea as needed.

Nutrition facts per serving:
Calories 218, total fat 2 g, carbs 51 g,
Protein 3 g, sodium 127 mg

Chocolate Protein

The best way to start your morning is with protein. Protein keeps you feeling full longer and has been shown to help control appetite throughout the day. While chia seeds and nut butter are helping you stay full, raw cocoa powder serves as a super-powerful antioxidant—all the more reason to indulge in this creamy chocolate smoothie!

Yields: 2 – Prep. Time: 5 min. – Cooking Time: 0 min.

Ingredients
2 bananas
1 cup soy milk
2 tablespoons chia seeds
2 tablespoons nut butter
2–3 tablespoons raw cocoa powder or chocolate protein powder
¼ teaspoon cinnamon

Preparation
1. Combine all ingredients and blend until smooth. Slowly add milk as needed.

Nutrition facts per serving:
Calories 339, total fat 15 g, carbs 48 g, Protein 10 g, sodium 80 mg

Nuts & Dates

Dates are not only sweet, but also a nutritional powerhouse bringing protein, iron, and B vitamins to the table. All these nutrients can be more difficult to get on a vegan diet, so be sure to add this smoothie to your day.

Yields: 2 – Prep. Time: 5 min. – Cooking Time: 0 min.

Ingredients
2 bananas
1 cup vegan nut milk
¾ cup walnuts
⅓ cup pistachios
6 dates, pitted
1 tablespoon flaxseed
1 teaspoon cinnamon
¼ teaspoon ginger powder
1 teaspoon vanilla extract
Ice

Preparation
1. Combine all ingredients and blend until smooth. Slowly add milk as needed.

Nutrition facts per serving:
Calories 308, total fat 21 g, carbs 30 g,
Protein 7 g, sodium 92 mg

Ayurvedic Smoothie

Both ginger and turmeric are powerful anti-inflammatories believed to help prevent cancer and other serious conditions. This smoothie does not call for ice, because Ayurvedic medicine, the yogic science of health and nutrition, recommends avoiding cold foods.

Yields: 2 – Prep. Time: 5 min. – Cooking Time: 0 min.

Ingredients
1 banana
½ teaspoon turmeric
¼ teaspoon ginger
1 cup vegan milk
1 tablespoon maple syrup

Preparation
1. Combine all ingredients and blend until smooth. Slowly add milk as needed.

Nutrition facts per serving:
Calories 125, total fat 2 g, carbs 24 g,
Protein 4 g, sodium 62 mg

Fig Shake

With their sweet and unique flavor, figs are one of the treasures of the Mediterranean. They're also loaded with fiber and are a good source of magnesium, a mineral needed for restful sleep.

Yields: 2 – Prep. Time: 5 min. – Cooking Time: 0 min.

Ingredients
8 figs
2 bananas
1 cup vegan milk
1 teaspoon cinnamon
¼ teaspoon ginger, ground
Pinch cardamom
1 tablespoon maple syrup
¼ cup granola
Ice

Preparation

1. Combine all ingredients, except for the granola, and blend until smooth. Slowly add milk as needed.
2. Add granola and blend for a few seconds.

Nutrition facts per serving:
Calories 380, total fat 3 g, carbs 86 g,
Protein 8 g, sodium 65 mg

Winter Blues

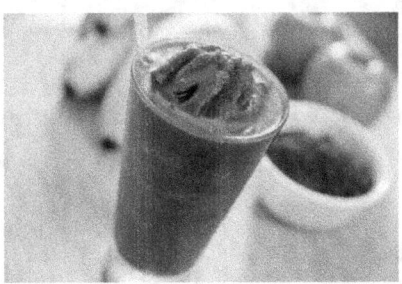

Seasonal Affective Disorder affects many of us. Luckily, there are ways to prevent the so-called winter blues. One of them is through diet. A diet high in omega-3 fatty acids, vitamin D, and probiotics can help you prevent winter depression, so add this smoothie to your routine come fall.

Yields: 2 – Prep. Time: 5 min. – Cooking Time: 0 min.

Ingredients
1 cup blueberries
1 packet acai puree
1 apple
1 cup vegan yogurt
1 tablespoon chia seeds
½ tablespoon flaxseeds
Ice

Preparation
1. Combine all ingredients and blend until smooth.

Nutrition facts per serving:
Calories 264, total fat 8 g, carbs 47 g,
Protein 5 g, sodium 27 mg

Green Smoothies

Pineapple-Mint

This smoothie is just so refreshing, a perfect addition to a summer day. Fresh mint helps to soothe your stomach, while pineapple is great for your skin. Anti-inflammatory pineapple has even been shown to help with arthritis pain. Another friend for your stomach, celery helps to prevent bloating, so drink this delicious smoothie before a hot date.

Yields: 2 – Prep. Time: 5 min. – Cooking Time: 0 min.

Ingredients
1½ cup pineapple
½ cup fresh mint leaves
1 stalk celery, diced
½ cup coconut water

Ice

Preparation
1. Combine all ingredients and blend until smooth. Slowly add ice and coconut water as needed.

Nutrition facts per serving:
Calories 173, total fat 0 g, carbs 44 g,
Protein 1 g, sodium 36 mg

Tummy Tamer

Probiotics from vegan yogurt combined with mint, ginger, and healthy fruits and veggies all work together to soothe your stomach. This smoothie can also work wonders for a bloated stomach.

Yields: 2 – Prep. Time: 5 min. – Cooking Time: 0 min.

Ingredients
1 cup vegan yogurt
½ cup coconut water
1 banana
½ cup pineapple
1 cup spinach
¼ cup mint leaves
½ lemon, juiced
1 tablespoon ginger, fresh
Ice

Preparation
1. Combine all ingredients and blend until smooth. Slowly add ice and coconut water as needed.

Nutrition facts per serving:
Calories 210, total fat 2 g, carbs 46 g,
Protein 5 g, sodium 42 mg

Tropical Greens

This smoothie delivers the gorgeous flavors and colors of the tropics, plus all the nutrients. Pineapple and papaya do wonders for your digestion, while coconut water delivers some much-needed electrolytes.

Yields: 4 – Prep. Time: 5 min. – Cooking Time: 0 min.

Ingredients
½ cup pineapple
½ cup papaya, peeled and diced
1 mango
1 banana
2 dates, pitted
1 cup spinach
1 cup kale
1 cup coconut water

Preparation
1. Combine all ingredients and blend until smooth. Slowly add ice and coconut water as needed.

Nutrition facts per serving:
Calories 174, total fat 1 g, carbs 44 g, Protein 1 g, sodium 108 mg

Herbal Remedy

Herbs are an overlooked green to add to smoothies! Not only are they packed with flavor, they're also full of vitamins and minerals. The herbs in this smoothie will especially help you to detox heavy metals from your system, while ginger serves as a diuretic, enhancing the detoxifying benefits.

Yields: 4 – Prep. Time: 5 min. – Cooking Time: 0 min.

Ingredients
1 green apple
1 cup pineapple
1 kiwi
2 dates, pitted
1 cup coconut water
1 cup spinach
½ cup cilantro
½ cup mint
1 tablespoon ginger
Ice

Preparation
1. Combine all ingredients and blend until smooth. Slowly add ice and coconut water as needed.

Nutrition facts per serving:
Calories 125, total fat <1 g, carbs 25 g,
Protein 1 g, sodium 24 mg

Strawberry Basil

Did you know that basil is antibacterial, antimicrobial, and anti-inflammatory? It's also filled with antioxidants and may help to prevent depression—all the more reason to try this unique and delicious smoothie!

Yields: 2 – Prep. Time: 5 min. – Cooking Time: 0 min.

Ingredients
1 cup strawberries
½ cup basil leaves, fresh
½ cup vegan milk
2 dates, pitted
Ice

Preparation
1. Combine all ingredients and blend until smooth. Slowly add ice and milk as needed.

Nutrition facts per serving:
Calories 68, total fat 1 g, carbs 13 g,

Protein 3 g, sodium 31 mg

Ginger Lime

With citrus lime and antibiotic ginger, this smoothie will work wonders for your immune system.

Yields: 2 – Prep. Time: 5 min. – Cooking Time: 0 min.

Ingredients
1 green apple
1 kiwi
2 limes, juiced
1 cup spinach
1 tablespoon ginger, fresh
2 dates, pitted
Water
Ice

Preparation
1. Combine all ingredients and blend until smooth. Slowly add ice and water as needed.

Nutrition facts per serving:
Calories 118, total fat <1 g, carbs 30 g,
Protein 2 g, sodium 16 mg

Creamy Greens

This smoothie is so creamy that it's practically ice cream. Avocado and banana deliver detoxifying fiber, while chia seeds add some protein and help you feel full. The perfect morning smoothie.

Yields: 2 – Prep. Time: 5 min. – Cooking Time: 0 min.

Ingredients
1 banana
1 avocado
1 cup pineapple
1 cup spinach
1 cup coconut water
2 dates
1 tablespoon chia seeds

Preparation
1. Combine all ingredients and blend until smooth. Slowly add ice and coconut water as needed.

Nutrition facts per serving:

Calories 347, total fat 13 g, carbs 60 g, Protein 4 g, sodium 52 mg

Green Tart

Some of us can't get enough of tart and tangy flavors. The tart green apples and vegan yogurt deliver all the flavor you need, while also working wonders for your digestive system. Meanwhile, limes and pomegranate seeds are here to support your immune system.

Yields: 2 – Prep. Time: 5 min. – Cooking Time: 0 min.

Ingredients
2 green apples
2 limes, juiced
1 cup vegan yogurt, plain
¼ cup pomegranate seeds
1 cup leafy greens
1 date, pitted
Ice

Preparation
1. Combine all ingredients and blend until smooth. Slowly add ice and coconut water as needed.

Nutrition facts per serving:
Calories 231, total fat 2 g, carbs 53 g,
Protein 5 g, sodium 28 mg

Morning Matcha

Matcha green tea isn't just one of the richest sources of antioxidants, it's also guaranteed to kick-start your morning. Avocado and coconut milk lend healthy fats that are great for your brain and skin and also help you feel full for hours. Drinking this smoothie in lieu of coffee will give you sustained energy all day.

Yields: 2 – Prep. Time: 5 min. – Cooking Time: 0 min.

Ingredients
2 teaspoons matcha powder
1 pear
1 cup pineapple
1 kiwi
½ avocado
½ cup spinach
1 cup coconut milk
Ice (if needed)

Preparation
1. Combine all ingredients and blend until smooth. Slowly add ice and coconut milk as needed.

Nutrition facts per serving:
Calories 376, total fat 20 g, carbs 50 g,
Protein 4 g, sodium 43 mg

Smoothie Bowls

Sunrise Smoothie Bowl

Smoothie bowls aren't just nutritious meals, they're works of art! This smoothie bowl combines tropical flavors and the beautiful color of the sunrise to help you start your morning.

Yields: 2 – Prep. Time: 5 min. – Cooking Time: 0 min.

Ingredients
½ cup papaya
½ cup pineapple
1 cup strawberries
1 banana, frozen
Coconut water (as needed)
1 tablespoon chia seeds
2 tablespoons coconut shreds

Preparation
1. Combine frozen banana with fruit and coconut water as needed. Blend until smooth.
2. Serve in a bowl topped with chia seeds, shredded coconut, and any other toppings you'd like.

Nutrition facts per serving:
Calories 348, total fat 6 g, carbs 76 g,
Protein 2 g, sodium 191 mg

Chocolate Mint Bowl

This mint chocolate chip smoothie bowl is so delicious that it's practically dessert. The good news is that raw cocoa powder is high in antioxidants, while fresh mint is soothing for your stomach and helps to reduce bloating.

Yields: 2 – Prep. Time: 5 min. – Cooking Time: 0 min.

Ingredients
2 bananas, frozen
Handful mint leaves
2 tablespoons cocoa powder
Vegan nut milk (as needed)
½ cup carob chips

Preparation

1. Add bananas, mint, and cocoa powder to your blender. Blend on high, adding nut milk a little at a time until you have your desired consistency.
2. Mix in carob chips and serve immediately.

Nutrition facts per serving:
Calories 239, total fat 7 g, carbs 49 g,
Protein 1 g, sodium 15 mg

Banana Split Bowl

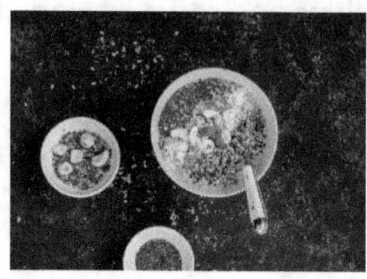

One of the best things about a vegan diet is that you can indulge all of your cravings without feeling guilty about it. Craving a banana split? No problem—try this delicious but healthy version.

Yields: 2 – Prep. Time: 5 min. – Cooking Time: 0 min.

Ingredients
2 bananas, frozen
1 banana
1 cup strawberries, plus extra for topping
Vegan whipped cream
Carob chips
Cherries
Almond milk (as needed)

Preparation
1. Add strawberries and frozen bananas to the blender. Blend together while slowly adding milk

until you reach your desired consistency. It should be thick, but not too thick.
2. Serve topped with cherries, whipped cream, carob chips, banana, and anything else you might like.

Nutrition facts per serving:
Calories 314, total fat 14 g, carbs 51 g,
Protein 4 g, sodium 40 mg

Nutella Bowl

Who doesn't love chocolate and hazelnuts? Instead of eating Nutella by the jar, try eating this healthy smoothie bowl instead. Nutella may not be the healthiest thing in the world, but hazelnuts are actually loaded with vitamin E, B vitamins, and healthy fats. This bowl is guaranteed to satisfy and nourish.

Yields: 2 – Prep. Time: 5 min. – Cooking Time: 0 min.

Ingredients
2 bananas, frozen
¼ cup hazelnuts
2 tablespoons cocoa powder
Vegan nut milk (as needed)
1 tablespoon maple syrup (or to taste)

Preparation

1. Blend all ingredients together, adding nut milk a little at a time until you have your desired consistency.

Nutrition facts per serving:
Calories 315, total fat 20 g, carbs 35 g,
Protein 7 g, sodium 39 mg

Ipanema Bowl

Acai bowls are one of the best things about Brazil. You can see Brazilians eating them by the beach and all over town. Not surprising, considering how delicious and nourishing these little purple berries are—super-high in antioxidants and a good source of omega fatty acids. You'll be feeling amazing after this smoothie bowl!

Yields: 2 – Prep. Time: 5 min. – Cooking Time: 0 min.

Ingredients
2 packs frozen acai pulp
2 bananas, frozen
1 mango
½ cup vegan milk
½ cup granola
Light agave nectar
Coconut shreds
3 strawberries, sliced

Preparation

1. Blend together the acai, mango, milk, and bananas until smooth.
2. Pour into a bowl and serve topped with agave nectar, strawberries, granola and shredded coconut.

Nutrition facts per serving:
Calories 446, total fat 13 g, carbs 81 g,
Protein 8 g, sodium 57 mg

Beauty Bowl

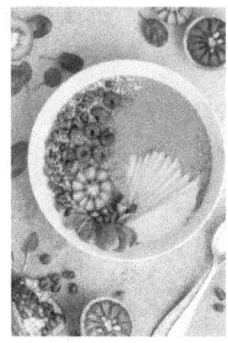

This yummy bowl is a filling meal that's also loaded with healthy fats and antioxidants to give you gorgeous, glowing skin.

Yields: 2 – Prep. Time: 5 min. – Cooking Time: 0 min.

Ingredients
2 bananas, frozen
1 pear
1 mango
1 cup spinach
2 tablespoons chia seeds
1 tablespoon nut butter
1 tablespoon flaxseed
Goji berries
Pomegranate seeds
Orange juice (as needed)

Preparations

1. Combine flaxseed, nut butter, spinach and fruit in the blender. Blend until smooth, adding orange juice as needed.
2. Serve in bowls topped with chia seeds, pomegranate seeds, and goji berries.

Nutrition facts per serving:
Calories 374, total fat 11 g, carbs 73 g,
Protein 9 g, sodium 62 mg

Ocean Breeze

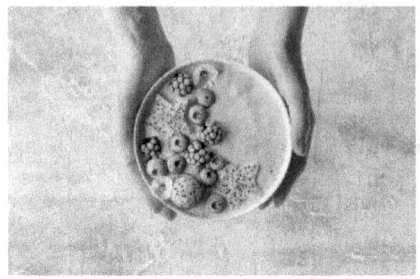

The health benefits of protein-packed spirulina cannot be overstated. Some have even called this algae the most nutrient-dense food on earth. Plus, this superfood gives this smoothie bowl a gorgeous color.

Yields: 2 – Prep. Time: 5 min. – Cooking Time: 0 min.

Ingredients
2 bananas, frozen
1 cup blueberries, plus more for topping
1 mango
Coconut water (as needed)
1 tablespoon chia seeds
1 teaspoon blue spirulina
Coconut shreds

Preparations
1. Combine fruit and spirulina in the blender. Blend until smooth, adding coconut water as needed.

2. Serve in bowls topped with chia seeds, coconut shreds, and more berries.

Nutrition facts per serving:
Calories 232, total fat 3 g, carbs 53 g,
Protein 4 g, sodium 5 mg

Strawberry Oatmeal

Loaded with protein and heart healthy fiber, oatmeal is the ideal breakfast. Add it to strawberries and banana in this super-simple smoothie bowl for a creamy, delicious meal.

Yields: 2 – Prep. Time: 5 min. – Cooking Time: 0 min.

Ingredients
2 bananas, frozen
1 cup strawberries, plus extra for topping
⅓ cup rolled oats
¼ teaspoon vanilla extract
1 tablespoon chia seeds
Almond milk (as needed)
Rose petals (optional)

Preparation
1. Combine fruit, oats, and vanilla in the blender. Blend until smooth, adding almond milk as needed.
2. Serve in bowls topped with chia seeds, more berries, and rose petals.

Nutrition facts per serving:
Calories 232, total fat 3 g, carbs 53 g,
Protein 4 g, sodium 5 mg

Turbo Greens Protein

Not everyone loves eating their greens, but they really are good for you! If you're one of those who'd rather avoid them, try eating them disguised in a delish smoothie! This smoothie is filled with vitamin C, antioxidants, and enough greens to get you through the day.

Yields: 2 – Prep. Time: 5 min. – Cooking Time: 0 min.

Ingredients
2 bananas, frozen
1 cup mixed berries, plus extra for topping
1 kiwi, peeled
1 cup spinach
1 cup kale, stems removed
¼ cup quinoa, cooked
2 dates, pitted
1 tablespoon nut butter
1 tablespoon flaxseed
2 tablespoons chia seeds

Soy milk (as needed)

Preparation
1. Combine fruit, nut butter, greens, and quinoa in the blender and blend until smooth, adding soy milk as needed.
2. Serve in bowls topped with chia seeds and berries.

Nutrition facts per serving:
Calories 317, total fat 8 g, carbs 60 g,
Protein 8 g, sodium 23 mg

Dragon Fruit Bowl

This exotic fruit is a work of art that's also filled with fiber, prebiotics, and vitamin C, so it's great for your digestive and immune systems. The beautiful bright pink color might even tempt some of the little ones into trying this bowl!

Yields: 2 – Prep. Time: 5 min. – Cooking Time: 0 min.

Ingredients
2 bananas, frozen
1 dragon fruit
1 star fruit, sliced
1 mango
2 tablespoons chia seeds
2 pineapple rings
Coconut shreds
Coconut water (as needed)

Preparation

1. In a blender, combine bananas, dragon fruit, and mango. Blend until smooth, adding coconut water as needed.
2. Serve in bowls topped with pineapple, chia seeds, star fruit, and coconut shreds.

Nutrition facts per serving:
Calories 356, total fat 13 g, carbs 66 g,
Protein 8 g, sodium 40 mg

Key Lime Pie Smoothie Bowl

Who says you can't have dessert for breakfast? This refreshing and indulgent breakfast smoothie bowl is a great way to supercharge your mornings.

Yields: 2 – Prep. Time: 5 min. – Cooking Time: 0 min.

Ingredients
3 tablespoons key lime juice
1 frozen banana
½ cup spinach
1 Granny Smith apple
1–2 tablespoons light agave nectar
Water

Preparation
1. Add the frozen banana to your blender and blend on low. Add water a tablespoon at a time, as needed, until the banana reaches a creamy consistency.

2. Add the remaining ingredients and blend again until creamy.

Nutrition facts per serving:
Calories 248, total fat <1 g, carbs 61 g,
Protein 2 g, sodium 0 mg

Dessert Smoothies

Cinnamon Roll

Cinnamon rolls in the morning are sure to get everyone out of bed fast, but they're also loaded with sugar and simple carbs that give you an energy crash by noon. This smoothie has oats that help you maintain your energy all day long.

Yields: 2 – Prep. Time: 5 min. – Cooking Time: 0 min.

Ingredients
1 banana, frozen
1 cup vegan milk
½ cup rolled oats
1 tablespoon maple syrup
½ teaspoon cinnamon, ground, plus extra for topping

½ teaspoon vanilla extract
Vegan whipped cream

Preparation
1. Combine all ingredients and blend until smooth.
2. Serve topped with cinnamon and/or whipped cream.

Nutrition facts per serving:
Calories 375, total fat 17g, carbs 50 g,
Protein 9 g, sodium 78 mg

Peaches and Cream

With this healthy, vitamin-C-packed smoothie, your skin will be as clear and creamy as peaches and cream.

Yields: 2 – Prep. Time: 5 min. – Cooking Time: 0 min.

Ingredients
2 peaches
1 cup vegan milk
⅓ cup rolled oats
1 tablespoon maple syrup
½ teaspoon vanilla extract
Pinch of cinnamon (optional)
Vegan whipped cream
Ice

Preparation

1. Combine all ingredients and blend until smooth.
2. Serve topped with cinnamon and whipped cream.

Nutrition facts per serving:
Calories 293, total fat 15 g, carbs 37 g,
Protein 5 g, sodium 76 mg

Autumn Delight

This smoothie is filled with fiber and probiotics, so it's a great addition to a cleanse or just a good way to lower cholesterol. Not to mention it captures all the delicious flavors of fall!

Yields: 2 – Prep. Time: 5 min. – Cooking Time: 0 min.

Ingredients
2 apples, Honeycrisp is best
2 pears
1½ cups vegan yogurt, plain
¼ cup granola
2 tablespoons maple syrup
1 teaspoon cinnamon, ground
¼ teaspoon ginger, ground
Vegan whipped cream

Preparation
1. Combine all ingredients, except for the granola, and blend until smooth. Slowly add milk as needed.

2. When the smoothie is blended to your desired consistency, add granola and pulse for a few seconds. You just want to mix it in a little.

Nutrition facts per serving:
Calories 583, total fat 16 g, carbs 110 g,
Protein 10 g, sodium 29 mg

Piña Colada

Piña colada is a tropical summer favorite. Serve this one around the pool and no one will have any idea it's filled with vitamin C and sugar free!

Yields: 2 – Prep. Time: 5 min. – Cooking Time: 0 min.

Ingredients
1 banana, frozen
1 cup pineapple
1 cup coconut yogurt, coconut flavor
1 tablespoon light agave nectar
Coconut shreds

Preparation
1. Combine all ingredients except for the coconut shreds and blend until smooth.
2. Serve topped with coconut shreds.

Nutrition facts per serving:
Calories 235, total fat <0 g, carbs 56 g,

Protein 5 g, sodium 41 mg

Strawberry Rosewater

Rosewater is soothing for the central nervous system and also good for your skin. If you suffer from morning anxiety, this smoothie is a delicious way to start your day off right.

Yields: 2 – Prep. Time: 5 min. – Cooking Time: 0 min.

Ingredients
1 cup strawberries
1 cup vegan yogurt, plain
½ cup pomegranate seeds
1–2 tablespoons rosewater
2 dates, pitted
Ice

Preparation
1. Combine all ingredients and blend until smooth. Add ice as needed.

Nutrition facts per serving:

Calories 148, total fat 2 g, carbs 31 g, Protein 4 g, sodium 15 mg

Gingerbread Smoothie

Gingerbread is a delightful holiday treat, but those of us who are gluten intolerant don't get to indulge. This smoothie is the solution. Plus, the warming spices and vegan yogurt are great for your digestion.

Yields: 2 – Prep. Time: 5 min. – Cooking Time: 0 min.

Ingredients
1 banana
1 cup vegan yogurt, plain
2 tablespoons molasses
1 teaspoon cinnamon
¼ teaspoon ginger, ground
1 pinch allspice
Ice

Preparation

1. Combine all ingredients and blend until smooth. Add ice as needed.

Nutrition facts per serving:
Calories 196, total fat 2 g, carbs 42 g,
Protein 4 g, sodium 21 mg

Pumpkin Pie Jar

Everyone loves sharing pumpkin pie around the holiday table, but did you know that pumpkin is actually loaded with vitamin A? That makes this smoothie a real treat for your skin as well as a delicious dessert.

Yields: 2 – Prep. Time: 5 min. – Cooking Time: 0 min.

Ingredients
1 banana, frozen
½ cup pumpkin puree
1 cup vegan milk, vanilla
1 tablespoon molasses
1 teaspoon pumpkin pie spices
Vegan whipped cream

Preparation
1. Combine all ingredients and blend until smooth.

Nutrition facts per serving:

Calories 282, total fat 14 g, carbs 37 g, Protein 6 g, sodium 67 mg

Hot Chocolate

Not all smoothies have to be cold! This warm smoothie is a healthier take on hot chocolate. Warm oats are guaranteed to give you sustained energy for hours.

Yields: 2 – Prep. Time: 8 hours – Cooking Time: 5 min.

Ingredients
1 cup vegan milk
½ cup rolled oats
2 tablespoons cocoa powder
1 tablespoon molasses

Preparation
1. Mix all ingredients together and allow to soak overnight in the fridge.
2. In the morning, add the ingredients to the blender and blend until smooth.
3. Heat in a saucepan and serve warm.

Nutrition facts per serving:
Calories 244, total fat 5 g, carbs 36 g,
Protein 10 g, sodium 60 mg

Chocolate Cherry

Come Valentine's Day, you may find yourself craving chocolate covered cherries. Why don't you try this vegan, sugar-free smoothie instead? Between cherries and cocoa powder, this smoothie is loaded with antioxidants, while healthy fats come courtesy of avocado.

Yields: 2 – Prep. Time: 5 min. – Cooking Time: 0 min.

Ingredients
1 cup sweet cherries, pitted
1 cup vegan milk
2 tablespoons raw cocoa
½ avocado
1 tablespoon maple syrup
Carob chips (optional topping)
Ice

Preparation
1. Combine all ingredients and blend until smooth.

Nutrition facts per serving:
Calories 265, total fat 8 g, carbs 46 g,
Protein 7 g, sodium 66 mg

Carrot Cake

Parents have long been using carrot cake to trick kids into eating their veggies. This smoothie is a super-easy vegan way to do the same. Carrots are loaded with vitamin A and fiber, while vegan yogurt and spices work wonders for your gut microbiome and overall digestive health.

Yields: 2 – Prep. Time: 5 min. – Cooking Time: 0 min.

Ingredients
1 banana
1 cup shredded carrots
1 cup vegan yogurt
2 tablespoons molasses
½ teaspoon cinnamon, ground
⅛ teaspoon ginger, ground
1 dash nutmeg
Water (as needed)
Ice (as needed)

Preparation
1. Combine all ingredients and blend until smooth.

Nutrition facts per serving:
Calories 240, total fat 2 g, carbs 52 g,
Protein 5 g, sodium 108 mg

Part 2

Introduction

We are what we eat. It's been said many times before and rightly so. The food that we eat, the air which we breathe and the water which we drink are the three most important ingredients that make our body healthy. Food choices are important as food nourishes the body, has an effect on our mood swings, appearance, weight, aging and our overall health and wellbeing.

Research indicates that the human skin gets replaced every thirty five days; the liver has the capacity to repair itself and re-grow and with the help of the blood supply, they clear the toxic waste out of the body. How well this key bodily function performs depends greatly on the food people choose to consume. Eat well and the body performs well i.e. balanced weight, sustained energy levels and a healthy immune system capable of fighting off infections and disease. Poor eating habits and you stand a good chance of the opposite, being a body under nourished, over weight, continually feeling sluggish or lethargic, high level of toxins in the system and ultimately a poor immune system not capable of fighting off sickness.

Food that is rich in nutrients, vitamins, fiber and minerals, along with having protein content and some antioxidant powers, should be consumed to maintain a healthy and balanced lifestyle. Processed foods, typically high in fat, calories, salt, sugar and artificial additives, offer very little in the way of essential nutrients and minerals the body needs. In most cases the processing of these foods takes energy from the body and disrupts the normal digestive process.

A balanced and proper diet is the basic principle to maintaining regular weight and toxin levels in the body. Natural foods are the best for this as they give the right amount of energy and minerals that the body needs. Fruits and vegetables are a key source of these vital nutrients and minerals as they have the quality of being able to detoxify as well as supporting natural weight loss.

However for most of us our hectic lifestyles means it's difficult to prepare our food in advance thereby most people just grab a bite of food whenever they find time. In most cases the wrong type of foods (did someone say Fast Food?)

This is where Smoothies and Juicing are able to assist. The reason they are so powerfully healthy for our bodies is because it's an extremely concentrated source of vital nutrients - it's basically packed with giant heaps of health in a blender! We would actually need to eat bucketfuls of fresh fruits and vegetables (2 lbs of carrots, 8 lbs, or more than half a stone of spinach, and 10-12 apples) to receive the same amount of vitamins and enzymes that are found in a 16 ounce (or 500 gram) serving of juice!

Drinking fresh juices and smoothies is one of the easiest and cheapest ways to significantly boost your immune system and improve all aspects of your health!

When you drink the smoothies, the highly concentrated vitamins, minerals and enzymes quickly enter your bloodstream, and become absorbed by the body instantly, rather than going through the long digestive process. This also gives your digestive organs the much-needed opportunity to finally rest. Juicing is also known to improve various aspects of our bodies, including skin conditions, weight-loss and liver function.

Therefore whether you're looking for ways to boost your skin's appearance, lose weight or treat various health conditions such as cardiovascular disease, drinking freshly blended smoothies can target all of these health concerns and leave you feeling (and looking!) amazing!

However before we dive right into the yummy 14 Nutrient-Packed Smoothies to Help You Detox, Lose Weight and Feel FantasticI've provided some background on natural weight loss, detoxification, food and their nutrients and the benefits of Smoothies.

Also as my way of saying thank you for downloading my book I've included a **Limited Time Bonus** right after the conclusion. I hope you get as much value from it as I have and trust you get real value from my book.

Ladies and Gentlemen—start your blenders!

Chapter 1: Losing Weight

Who does not want to look slim? In the current era, appearance is given more importance than being fit and healthy. There is no harm in toning down your body to look perfectly curvy, slim and sleek. However, it should be kept in mind during this race for perfection that peopleshouldn't forget to choose the healthy way of losing weight. Being overweight is also a big risk as it causes lots of health problems. So maintaining a healthy weight is vital.

The healthy way of losing weight can be a slower process than quick methods of slimming down, but it is the right choice in the longer run. It will help you to get rid of the excess weight permanently and maintain your ideal weight. This involves a change in your lifestyle with strict control on the diet and regular exercise. Balanced diet and exercise go hand in hand. So, by skipping either of these, the plan will not work.

Plan the weight loss

First, plan your weight loss by preparing a target and time schedule to achieve the target. Prepare a calorie chart stating how much weight you want to lose in a week. One pound of weight equals 3500 calories. Based on this calculation, plan the calorie intake for the week. Don't be too strict with the diet plan. Eat what satisfies you by making smart selections; there is no point in starving or feeling unhappy and cranky, thereby discontinuing the entire plan before it gets started.

Balanced diet

With your busy life, you hardly take time out to eat properly. You just grab a quick bite of junk, a burger or some ready-to-eat food. These will not help you to lose your weight nor do they give you enough nutrition to maintain your body correctly.

A diet which consists of a list of foods, preferably made with natural and fresh vegetables and fruits, rich in minerals and vitamins, and religiously following it daily, is the proper way to maintain your balanced weight. The food should contain all the nutrients in the right proportions with low calories to be considered as being part of a balanced diet.

Exercise/yoga

Exercise/yoga is the effort people put in to moving their body parts, giving them strength, stamina and flexibility. This keeps all the body parts active and toned. Exercise is like a medicine to lubricate the wear and tear caused to the body parts in your day to day life.

Losing weight involves being within limits, i.e. a restrictive diet. Do not deny your temptations; just make sure you eat less of the unhealthy food when you are tempted by it. Avoid eating all the time, eat only the required amount and at specified intervals as per your plan.

Foods that assists natural weight loss

Water is a magic item that helps in the smooth functioning of your body. Even for weight loss, it helps to a great extent by allowing you to eat less than what is actually required. With this logic, it is advisable to take in all the fruits and vegetables that contain a higher level of water. Here's some food tips to get you started:

- Black beans are protein rich.
- Oats boost metabolism and burn fat.
- Avocados are fiber rich and fill the stomach and reduce hunger.
- Salmon (low fat meat) and eggs have high protein that helps you to stay full longer.
- Broccoli and green tea contain antioxidants, which prevent cancer growth and also help in maintaining weight.
- Brown rice is fiber rich, giving high energy and low calories.
- Pears and watermelons contain a high level of water, and are extremely helpful for weight loss.
- Grape fruit, wine, tofu, high fiber cereals, cucumber, red pepper, kidney beans, lentils, almonds, pine nuts, olive oil, white beans, low fat milk, barley, plantains, banana are some of the foods which can help in natural weight loss process.

Chapter 2: All You Need to Know About Detox

In this chapter, we will help you to understand what detox is and what effects it has on your body

What is detox?

It is a process by which living organisms remove the toxic and harmful substances from their bodies. There are so many chemical substances and acids that get generated inside the human body, and they will cause harm to the body long term.

It is better to get rid of these unwanted chemicals and acids (both artificial and natural), in order to stay healthy and feel fresh.

There are several procedures for detoxification, but the natural way is always the best. It has been proven that people feel more energetic and active following the detox diet.

Detoxing helps in taking the toxic load out of the body organs. All the organs of your body like the stomach, liver, bowel, kidney etc. work regularly without a break causing wear and tear. The detoxification process helps the organs to recoup themselves with energy and clean the respective organs for better and healthier functioning in the future. This can be done by giving it a less heavy load or giving some rest to the organs by giving them low calorie, easily digestible food.

Foods that assist in cleansing and detoxifying your body

Here is a list of some of the fruits and vegetables that will help in detoxing the body in a healthy and natural way.

1. Artichokes and asparagus help in building good bacteria in the body, thereby providing immunity.

2. **Oranges and other citrus fruits behave as natural antioxidants, providing vitamin C and producing glutathione for detoxification of liver.**

3. Brussels sprouts / broccoli /cabbage / cauliflower are high in fiber and help in improving gut, kidney and liver function.

4. **Sweet potatoes, lentils and beans are rich in Vitamin –B and zinc that maintains and takes care of digestion, functioning of cells and metabolism.**

5. **Oats are fiber rich and help to fuel the liver by removing deadly bile and addresses the growth of short chain fatty acid.**

6. Yogurt, avocado, beets, apple, Brazil nuts, cilantro, cinnamon, cranberries, garlic, ginger, fennel, flex seeds, grape tea, lemon grass, olives, pineapples, parsley, onions, melons, coconut etc., are some of the foods having their own characteristics to help you detox naturally by providing the protection needed.

Chapter 3: Food and Nutrition

There are so many of benefits of food that intake of the wrong food can cause various diseases and death in the long run. There is an old saying which proves perfect for demonstrating this,"let food be your medicine and medicine be your food". Right food rightly taken can save you from many diseases and also helps you to be fresh, healthy and strong.

For a long, healthy life there are so many things one needs to take account of, food being a part of it that plays a vital role. Apart from exercise, limited or no smoking and drinking, as well as less stress, what we eat and how we eat it is a crucial factor in maintaining healthy lifestyle to feel fantastic.

Three main nutrition components are protein, carbohydrates and fat. All these three should be taken in right proportions, through various foods and in a controlled manner, for maintaining health physically and mentally. Apart from this, we cannot ignore the need for vitamins and minerals which have their own contribution in body functioning.

Healthy eating habits involve healthy preparation and storage of food that saves the nutritional values and lessens the illness caused by incorrect cooking and preparation methods, as well as incorrect preservation of foods.

Energy can be gained by a healthy start to the day by having fruit for breakfast which gives instant energy. A diet should exclude sugar, and use fat to maintain blood sugar fluctuations. Carbohydrates should be included as they have more nutritional value. Meals should be taken at equal intervals of time.

Bone and teeth can be taken care of by consuming the required amount of calcium through milk, yoghurt, cheese, cereals and vegetables like broccoli. The benefit of calcium can be gained only when it gets absorbed in your body, and vitamin D helps in the absorption of calcium in your body.

The heart is the most important part of the body that requires utmost care. Low cholesterol, sodium and fat in the diet can reduce the chance of heart disease. i.e. fried foods, packed and processed foods, coconut oil, palm oil are few food items which should be avoided or consumed less in order to maintain a healthy heart.

The brain is a vital part of the body that works only through the nutrition that goes to it through the blood circulation. The better the nutrition, more the blood flow and less chance of brain diseases like Alzheimer. Food rich in vitamin E increases the memory power as well as helps in fighting Alzheimer. Spinach, broccoli, nuts, walnuts, raisins, blueberries, raspberries, prunes etc. are some of the foods which should be added into the regular diet

Natural Methods for Weight loss and Detoxification

With several methods available, these are proven to be the best and help in quick detoxification and also in the weight loss process.

Fruit diet:

Being on a fruit diet for a day or two a week or following it for a week maximum, helps in the detoxification process and also provides the required energy and minerals. It also helps in managing weight and reduces the chances of heart attacks. Plan the diet with the fruits of your choice. Either one variety of fruit or a fruit platter, everything is effective. Choices of fruits should be made in the right way, i.e. fruits with highest detoxification power should be consumed like oranges, lemon and grapes which are high on vitamin C, potassium and resveratrol should be included.

Liquid diet:

This is a short term method to be followed for the maximum of two days. The diet is limited to juices (fruits and vegetables), water, teas, protein shakes etc. All the minerals should be planned and taken in the rightquantity so that you don't get low on energy. Here, fruit and vegetable juices give required minerals and water/ teas help in losing weight.

Vegetables and Fruits diet:

This is a seven day diet program with fruits and vegetables that contains minerals required by the body. Here are a few food names to help in planning your balanced fruit and vegetable diet.

1. Kidney beans, soya beans, black beans, sprouts, apple, blueberries can be taken for fiber.
2. Carrots, squash, apricot, sweet potatoes, banana, can be taken for potassium.

3. Kiwi, tomatoes, mangoes, orange, bell pepper, Brussels sprouts, strawberries can take care of vitamin C requirement.
4. Spinach, oranges, peas, asparagus, melons can be taken to maintain folate.
5. **Olive and coconut give required amount of fat.**

Water is the most important and does wonders in maintaining a toned and fit body. It flushes out the toxic liquid from the blood like urea, nitrogen and thereby maintaining the fluid level inside your body. Drinking plain water can be a pain sometimes, so you can add flavor to it by having lemon juice or orange juice. Juices with citric acid help to reduce fat intake. Ideally, a minimum of two to three liters of water intake per day is beneficial.

Food to avoid while losing weight and detoxification

In our day to day life people consume so many foods that are unhealthy and that can have a reverse effect on their bodies. Temptations never end, and controlling them can be even tougher. One slip from the healthy diet and the entire efforts with your diet, exercise and controlled lifestyle can appear to be wasted.

A few foods are very dangerous and can have immediate adverse effect.

1. By drinking water instead of soda on a daily basis, there are chances of losing around 30-32 pounds in a year.

2. Forms of alcohol, being processed drinks, lower your body's metabolism by 70%.
3. Whole grain food is better and more beneficial than multi grain food.
4. **Fast food, table sugar, cakes, gum, candy, plain jam, sweets, pudding, syrups, pickles, salted nuts, coffee, sodas, baked food with white flour, bottled food, popcorns etc. can make you fat twice as fast as you slimmed down.**

For detoxification, solid foods should be consumed and any of these foods should be completely avoided:

Dairy products, peanuts, soybean products, butter, mayonnaise, corn, barley, caffeine, soda, processed oils, animal protein, creamed vegetables, chocolates, ketchups, chutneys, honey etc.

Chapter 4: Smoothies and Their Benefits

Eating the required amount of fresh fruits and vegetables to maintain your body daily, in its raw state, can be a bit boring. To make it interesting and appealing, you can modify them in the form of a smoothie and drink, thereby satisfying your daily nutrition dose.

Smoothies are a drink blended with fresh fruits and vegetables, yoghurt, ice-cream, milk, ice, honey, syrups etc. All the ingredients are high in minerals, fiber, protein and vitamins thereby making it healthier than a normal drink.

Having a control on the ingredients and calorie content, you can make the smoothie with your choice of fruits and vegetables. It is fully natural and has many health benefits.

Why smoothies?

- It can be prepared quickly.
- It helps you in detoxifying your system.
- It helps to make the immune system better.
- It looks appealing and tempting.
- It can be consumed quickly.
- It keeps you full for a longer time.
- It keeps the calorie intake in check.
- It is nutrient packed, and helps to maintain the diet and energy.

Chapter 5: Nutrient-packed smoothie recipes

And now, the section I'm sure you've really been waiting for - 14 Nutrient-Packed Smoothies to Help You Detox, Lose Weight and Feel Fantastic. Enjoy!

Smoothies for slimming down
The green punch

This smoothie gives you more than the required amount of minerals and vitamins for your diet. With Vitamin C, calcium and magnesium in it, it serves as a perfect drink for taking care of all the body's requirements also serves as an antioxidant dosage.

Serves – 2 Cups

Ingredients

- 1 medium sized banana
- 2 cups of papaya
- 1 medium green apple
- 1 cup spinach
- 1 cup kale

Method

1. Wash spinach thoroughly with water, and blend it well
2. Slice banana, papaya, kale and green apple into small pieces and add to the mix and blend it again.
3. For changing the consistency of the liquid, a little amount of water can be added based on your requirements.

Soy Smoothie

This smoothie, with around 300 calories, is a quick drink and helps you to lose weight with the help of soya, coconut water and almonds and has high nutritional value.

Serves – 3-4 Cups

Ingredients
- 4 tbsp. flax seeds
- 4 tbsp. pumpkin seeds
- 4 tbsp. sesame seeds
- 4 tbsp. sunflower seeds
- 2 cup of soya milk (unflavored)
- 1.5 cup coconut water
- 2 teaspoon salt (Himalayan crystal)
- 8 tbsp. almonds

Method
1. Take the sunflower seeds, flax seeds, sesame seeds and pumpkin seeds in a pan and dry roast them in low flame. Be careful as they can get burnt in a split second.
2. Let the seeds cool for a while.
3. Now grind the seeds to coarse powder and add coconut water.
4. Slice the almonds into small rough pieces.
5. Add the blended mix to soya milk and heat on a low flame for 2-4 minutes.
6. Serve it in a glass with almonds sprinkled on top.
7. If the consistency is very liquid, then reduce the quantity of coconut water to it.

8. To make it thicker you can use fresh coconut cream also. (Coconut cream is prepared by blending coconut flesh with a little amount of water.)

Cinnamon apple punch

A drink rich with protein, fat and which also has natural sugar. This helps you to keep your stomach full for longer. The best part is you can prepare and store it in the fridge at night and can have it in the morning for breakfast.

Serves – 3-4 Cup

Ingredients
- 2 medium sized apple
- 8 almonds (raw)
- 2 tbsp. cinnamon powder
- 2 tbsp. flax seeds
- 2 tbsp. regular vanilla extracts
- 10 ounce/300 ml of coconut water
- 2 tbsp. protein powder

Method
1. Clean, peel and slice apple into small pieces. Make sure sliced apple is approximately 2 cups.
2. Put all the ingredients into a blender and pulse it thoroughly.
3. Mix water to get desired consistency.
4. Sprinkle some cinnamon powder and finely chopped almonds on top of the smoothie before serving.
5. If you are going to have it in the morning, then let the smoothie be a little more liquid as it will solidify and become thick when refrigerated for the whole night, because of flax seeds.

Asparagus smoothie

This smoothie is rich with vitamin B1 (Thiamine), Vitamin B2 (Riboflavin), Vitamin B3 (Niacin), Vitamin B6 (Pyridoxine), B9 (Folate), Vitamin C, E, Copper, Zinc. This will help in quick increase in the various vitamin levels.

Serves – 1 - 2 Cups

Ingredients
- 1 cup of asparagus
- 1 cups of tomatoes
- 1 tbsp. of pumpkin seeds
- ½ tbsp. Himalayan crystal salt
- 1 cup coconut milk
- ½ cup coconut water

Method
1. Clean asparagus thoroughly in running water; keep it in boiling water for a while.
2. Take the asparagus from water and allow it to cool.
3. Slice tomatoes and asparagus once it cools and blend it well.
4. Filter the blended mix and take the juice out of it into a glass.
5. Now add salt, coconut milk and water to it and mix well.
6. Dry roast pumpkin seed mildly.
7. Slice the seeds into small pieces and sprinkle on top of the smoothie.
8. Ice cubes can be used while blending tomatoes and asparagus if you want the smoothie cold.

Banana with berries punch

This is a quick, easy to prepare smoothie which is ready in 5-7 minutes if the blender and ingredients are available. This smoothie contains less than 300 calories in a drink format and has vitamin B1, Vitamin B6, copper, magnesium, potassium, Vitamin K and phosphorus. Almond milk makes the smoothie taste delicious also giving nutrition value to it.

Serves – 2 Cups

Ingredients
- 1 cup of blueberries
- 16 ounce/500 ml of almond milk (Preferably homemade)
- 4 tbsp. of chia seeds
- 2 tbsp. of cocoa powder
- 10 strawberries
- 2 medium sized bananas pealed

Method
1. Clean the berries properly and put the berries and banana in the blender and pulse nicely.
2. Now add cocoa powder, chia seeds and almond milk to the blender and blend well.
3. You can add some water if the smoothie is very thick in consistency before serving.
4. Instead of chia seeds, flex seeds can be used.
5. **Cocoa powder, which is an antioxidant, can also be used instead of cocoa powder.**

Green spinach smoothie

This is a smoothie with a calorie level of 250-300 calories gives a perfect start keeping you full most of the day. It is a protein rich drink with fat and fiber contained in it.

Serves – 2 Cup

Ingredients
- 1 ½ cup of Greek yoghurt
- 1 1/2 pear (ripped)
- 2 tbsp. of fresh lime
- 4 tbsp. of avocado chopped
- 30 red grapes
- 4 cups of spinach leaves

Method

Wash spinach properly in running water.
1. Boil spinach in water for 5 minutes and then drain the water from it.
2. Alternatively, you can also steam spinach.
3. **Peel the pear, core and chop it into small pieces.**
4. Clean the grapes.
5. Now blend the yoghurt in the blender until it becomes creamy and then add the pear, avocado, spinach to it and blend it well.
6. Add lemon juice and pulse it twice.
7. Here, you can use green grapes also instead of red grapes.
8. Use fat-free unflavored yoghurt for better taste.

Low calorie vitality smoothie

This is a smoothie with a calorie level of 150-200 calories is a perfect for a healthy diet plan.

Serves – 1 Cup

Ingredients
- 4 Ounce/100 grams of Greek yoghurt
- 1 medium sized banana
- 1 tbsp. of cocoa powder
- 1 tbsp. of peanut butter
- One pinch of cinnamon
- 2 small sized ice cubes (If required)

Method
1. Put Greek yoghurt, cocoa powder, peanut butter and ice cubes (if required) or plain water half cup and blend it well,
2. Slice banana into small pieces and add to the mix and blend it again.
3. For making the consistency more liquid, a small amount of water can be added based on your requirement.
4. **Once you put the smoothie into a cup, put a pinch of cinnamon powder on top of it for garnishing and adding flavor to it.**

Smoothies for detoxification

Cherry berry smoothie

This is a smoothie with less than 150 calories helps to generate detoxifying enzymes and also helps with digestion process.

Serves – 2 Cups

Ingredients
- 2 cup raspberries (frozen)
- 1/2 cup of pitted cherries
- 4 tbsp. ginger (finely peeled and chopped)
- 2 tbsp. flax seeds
- 2 tbsp. lemon juice
- 1 ½ cup of almond milk
- 2-3 tbsp. of honey

Method
1. Wash the berries properly
2. Mix all the ingredients in the blender and blend well until it is a smooth liquid
3. You can use rice milk also instead of almond milk.
4. **Unsweetened berries give a better taste and are healthier to consume.**

Green veggie smoothie

This is a smoothie with less than 200 calories, and has high iron and zinc. It is a mix of fruits and vegetable and is very appealing with lots of vitamins and minerals. Here organic fruits and vegetables are beneficial as it can save us from pesticide intakes.

Serves – 2 -3 Cups

Ingredients
- 1.5 cups pure water
- 1 cup of apple
- 1 cup avocado
- 1cup of spinach leaves
- ½ cup of cucumber
- 1 – 2 celery stalk
- 4 Spring mint leaf
- 2 cups kiwi
- 1 tbsp. of lemon juice

Method
1. Wash the spinach in running water thoroughly.
2. Blend spinach in blender to smooth paste and then add other ingredients.
3. Once the mixture is smooth then pour it in cup and add lemon juice, mix well and serve.

Fruit cracker smoothie

This is a smoothie with 150-200 calories, rich in protein and fiber. Fruits like mango and kale provide required nutrition in our diet.

Serves – 3-4 Cups

Ingredients
- 2.5 cups of mango (frozen and sliced)
- 2.5 cups of kale leaf (Lacinato preferred)
- 3-4 medium sized ribs celery
- 1 cup of orange juice
- ½ cup of mint leaf (chopped)
- ½ cup of leaf parsley (chopped)

Method
1. Wash the kale and leave it in running water and remove the stem and tough ribs from it.
2. Add all the ingredients into a blender and blend well until it has a smooth liquid consistency.
3. Add water to change the consistency if required.
4. Fresh tangerine juice can be used in place of orange juice.

Carrot pepperonia smoothie

This is a smoothie with less than 150 calories which has the capacity to cure high blood pressure. It helps to loosen the arterial muscles thereby saving your heart from high blood pressure.

Serves – 2 Cups

Ingredients
- 4 medium sized carrots
- 1 large red bell peppers
- 2 medium sized tomatoes
- 3-4 garlic cloves
- ½ red jalapeno (seeded)
- 2-3 celery stalk
- ½ cup spinach leaf
- 1/2 cup water cross

Method
1. Wash the spinach in running water.
2. Slice carrots, tomatoes and bell peppers.
3. Blend spinach in blender to a smooth paste and then add other ingredients.
4. Once the mixture is smooth then pour it in a cup.
5. **You can blend it with ice cubes to serve it cold.**

Coconut cucumber smoothie

This is a smoothie with less than 120 calories. It is a thin smoothie that helps in detoxification of skin giving a clear glowing skin. The ingredients are high on oxygenating, rejuvenating, nourishing and toning the skin. This smoothie has vitamins A and C that reduce oily skin and helps the skin tissues to strengthen.

Serves – 2 Cups

Ingredients
- 2 cucumbers
- 2 apples
- 2 limes
- 2 cup coconut kefir
- 1cup of flat-leaf parsley
- 2 tbsp. of coconut oil
- 4 tbsp. fresh mint leaf (finely chopped)

Method
1. Wash the parsley in water and take off the leaves and stem for making the smoothie.
2. **Blend all the ingredients in the blender and pour it into water once it is finely blended.**
3. Add the chopped mint leaves on top before serving.

Ginger spin smoothie

This is a low calorie smoothie that gives anti-inflammatory benefits. This helps in taking care of the congestion, digestion and gas problems. This is a spicy drink that will awaken the taste buds.

Serves – 2 Cups

Ingredients
- 2 nubs ginger root
- 2 cups of spinach leaves
- 1.5 cups of pure water
- 2 tbsp. of cinnamon
- 2 tbsp. of chopped mint leaves

Method
1. Wash the spinach thoroughly in running water and chop it.
2. **Wash and mince the ginger.**
3. Add all the ingredients to the blender and mix well till it becomes a smooth liquid.
4. Pour the liquid into a cup and serve with mint leaves on top 0f it.

Avocado lime smoothie

This smoothie gives your body potassium, magnesium, vitamin C, for cleansing the kidneys.

Serves – 2 Cups

Ingredients
- 2 cups pure water
- 2 bananas
- 1 avocado
- 1 lime
- ½ cup of cucumber
- 2 kiwis
- ½ cup of walnuts

Method
1. Wash and peel avocado, lemon and kiwi.
2. **Mix all the ingredients together in a blender and blend well. Serve in a cup.**
3. Walnuts are optional and can be left out if not required.
4. One cup of thoroughly washed and chopped spinach/ kale can also be added to this drink.

Pacific Smoothie

Ingredients

- Ice cubes (10)
- Banana (1 large)
- Brown sugar (4 tsp)
- Eggnog (1 cup)
- Orange juice (1/4 cup)
- Maple syrup (4 tsp)
- Yogurt (1/4 cup)

Direction

Combine all the ingredients and blend for 3 minutes until completely blend. Pour into glasses and serve.

Penny's Smoothie

Ingredients

- Frozen peach slices (3/4 cup)
- Yogurt (1/4 cup)
- All fruit blueberries syrup (2 tbsp)
- Banana (1 large)

- Frozen Blueberries (1/4 cup)
- Rice milk (1/8 cup)

Direction

Combine Rice milk, blueberries syrup, yogurt, frozen peach slices, frozen blueberries and banana and blend them. Pour into glasses and serve this yummy smoothie.

Banana strawberry Smoothie

Ingredients

- Strawberries (1 cup, fresh)
- Ice cream (1 ½ cup)
- Ice cubes (1 ½ cups)
- Milk (half cup)
- Banana (1 large)
- Fresh peaches (1 cup)
- Apple (1 cup)

Direction

Combine the ingredients, milk, ice cubes, ice cream apple, fresh peaches, banana and strawberries and blend them well. Pour into glasses and serve.

Fig Smoothie

Ingredients

- Frozen bananas (2 large, peeled and cut into chunks)
- Orange juice (3/4 cup)
- Fig (6 fresh, halved)
- Milk (3/4 cup)

Direction

Combine all the four ingredients and blend them well. Pour into glasses and serve this yummy smoothie. Enjoy this one with your family to share happiness.

Orange Smoothie

Ingredients

- Concentrated orange juice (1 can about 6 ounce, frozen)
- Water (1 cup)
- White sugar (1/3 cup)
- Ice cubes (10)
- Milk (1 cup)

Direction

Combine all the ingredients along with orange juice and give it few high speed pulses. Blend until completely smooth. Pour into glasses and serve.

All Around Good Smoothie

Ingredients

- Powdered protein supplement (2 tbsp)
- Flax seed (1 ½ tbsp)
- Milk (half cup)
- Plain yogurt (half cup)
- Banana (half, frozen, peeled and chopped)
- Honey (1 tsp)

•Frozen strawberries (half cup)

Direction

Combine all the ingredients to the blender bowl and blend until completely smooth. Blend for atleast two minutes and pour it into glasses. Serve this yummy recipe.

Pumpkin Smoothie

Ingredients

•Brown sugar (1/4 cup)

•Ground cinnamon (2 tsp)

•Pumpkin puree (1 can about 16 ounce)

•Milk (2 cups)

Direction

Add the pumpkin to oven and switch to high heat until get soften. Add brown sugar, pumpkin, milk and cinnamon to the blender and blend it well. Give it few high speed pulses and pour into glasses. Serve this special smoothie.

Razzy Blue Smoothie

Ingredients

- Flaxseed meal (1 tbsp)
- Frozen blueberries (1 cup)
- Rolled oats (1/4 cup)
- Concord grape juice (1/4 cup)
- Buttermilk (1 cup, one percent)
- Raspberry yogurt (1 cup)
- Banana (1)
- Whole almonds (16)

Direction

Combine the frozen banana with all the other ingredients and give it few high speed pulses. Pour into glasses and serve it well.

Refreshing Smoothie

Ingredients

- Pineapple chunck (half can about 16 ounce, undrained)

- Strawberries (5 frozen)

Direction

Combine both of the ingredients to the blender bowl and blend it completely. Pour into glasses and serve.

Key lime pie smoothie

Ingredients

- Banana (1 frozen, cut into chunk)
- Ice cubes (1 ½ cup, crushed)
- Orange juice (1 splash)
- Greek yogurt (1 container about 6 ounce, key lime flavored)
- Heavy whipping cream (1 tbsp)

Direction

Combine all the ingredients to the blender and blend them well until completely smooth. Pour into glasses and serve.

Afternoon Smoothie

Ingredients

- Milk (1 cup)
- Mango (1/3, peeled, seeded and diced)
- Strawberries (4, hulled)
- Honey (3 tsp)
- Peach yogurt (1/4 cup, low fat)

Direction

Combine all the ingredients to the blender and blend it completely until smooth. Pour into glasses and serve.

Rosy Ginger peach Smoothie

Ingredients

- Fresh peach (1, sliced)
- Strawberry flavored yogurt (1 container about 6 ounce)
- Strawberries (half cup)
- Honey (1 tbsp)
- Milk (half cup)

- Ground ginger (1/8 tsp)

Direction

Combine all the ingredients to the blender jar and blend it completely. Blend every ingredient to the ground level and pour into glasses and serve.

Watermelon Smoothie

Ingredients

- Ice cubes (2 cups)
- Watermelon (1, cut into cubes and seeded)
- White sugar (half cup)
- Spearmint leaves (2 or more for taste)

Direction

Combine all the four ingredients to the blender and blend completely until smooth. Pour into glasses and serve.

Black and Blueberry Smoothie

Ingredients

- Blueberries (half cup, frozen)
- Coconut butter (2 tbsp)
- Honey (1 tbsp)
- Almond milk (1 cup, unsweetened)
- Blackberries (half cup, frozen)
- Chia seeds (1 tbsp)

Direction

Combine all the ingredients to the blender bowl and blend until completely smooth. Pour into glasses and serve it.

Tasty Strawberries Smoothie

Ingredients

- Ground oats (1/4 cup)
- Milk (3/4 cup, low fat)
- Strawberry yogurt (1 container about 6 ounce)
- Strawberries (half cup, frozen)
- Flax seed meal (1 tsp)

Direction

Combine Flax seed meal, Ground oats, strawberries, strawberries yogurt and milk to the blender jar and blend it completely. Blend until completely smooth. Pour into glasses and serve this yummy smoothie.

Coconut Banango Smoothie

Ingredients

- Coconut extract (1 tsp)
- Bananas (1 ½ frozen, sliced)
- Mango (1, peeled, seeded and chopped)
- Ice cubes (4)
- Cold water (half cup)
- White sugar (1 tbsp)
- Coconut milk (half cup)
- Lime zest (half tsp)

Direction

Combine zest, coconut extract, sugar, ice cubes, coconut milk, ice cubes, bananas to the blender bowl and blend it completely. Blend once again for 1 minute and pour into glasses and serve yummy smoothie.

Amaretto Smoothie

Ingredients

- amaretto liqueur (4 jiggers about of 1.5 ounce fluid)
- milk (4 jigger about 1.5 ounce fluid)
- Ice cream (1 cup)

Direction

Combine all the three ingredients and blend them. Pour into glasses and serve this yummy recipe.

BFF Smoothie

Ingredients

- Frozen strawberries (1 cup)
- Fresh mint leaves (5 or more according to taste)
- Plain greek yogurt (1 cup)

- Frozen mango chunks (1 cup)
- Milk (half cup, one percent)

Direction

Add protein powder, greek yogurt, strawberries, milk and mango and blend until smooth. Now add mint leaves and give few high speed pulses again and pour into glasses and serve.

Cinnapear Smoothie

Ingredients

- Pears (2, quartered and cores are removed)
- Banana (1 large and cut into chunks)
- Milk (1 cup)
- Yogurt (half cup)
- Ground cinnamon (half tsp)
- Ground nutmeg (1 pinch)

Direction

Combine the ingredients and add them to the blender jar. Blend it completely and pour into glasses and serve.

Tofuberry smoothie

Ingredients

- Raspberries (half cup)
- Silken tofu (1/4 cup, diced)
- Soy milk (2 tbsp)
- Fruit yogurt (1/4 cup)
- Banana (1/4)
- Orange juice (2 cups)

Direction

Combine orange juice, banana, raspberries, yogurt, soy milk and tofu to the blender and blend until smooth. Give 3-5 pulses. Pour into glasses and serve.

Gator Smoothie

Ingredients

- Ice cream (2 scoop)
- Ice cubes (2 cups)
- Grape flavored sports drink (2 cups)

Direction

Combine ice cream, sport drink and ice to the blender and blend until smooth. Pour into glasses and serve.

Sour Smoothie

Ingredients

- Ice cubes (1 cup)
- Kiwi (1, peeled)
- Lemon (1, peeled)
- Honey (1 tsp or more for taste)
- Orange (1, peeled)
- Lime (2, peeled)

Direction

Combine kiwi, honey, lemon, limes, orange and ice to the blender and blend until smooth. Pour into glasses and serve.

Milk and banana smoothie

Ingredients

- Low granulated sugar substitute (5 packets about 1 gram)

- Milk (1 cup)
- Bananas (1 ½)

Direction

Combine all the ingredients in a small bowl and blend them in high pulse blender. Pour into the glasses and serve.

All-fruit Smoothie

Ingredients

- Banana (1 large, cut into chunks)
- Pineapple juice (1 cup)
- Frozen strawberries (1 cup)
- Blueberries (1 cup, frozen)

Direction

Combine all the ingredients in the bowl and blend them in smoothie blender. Give it few high speed pulses. Chill and pour into glasses and serve.

Fruit and yogurt smoothie

Ingredients

- Milk (1 tsp)
- White sugar (1 ½ tsp)
- Pineapple juice (1/4 cup)
- Banana (1 large)
- Yogurt (half cup)
- Orange juice (1 tsp)
- Strawberries (1 cup)

Direction

Combine all the ingredients in blender bowl and give it few high speed pulses. Pour into glasses and serve.

Raspberry Banana Smoothie

Ingredients

- Orange juice (1 cup)
- Banana (1 large, cut into chunks)
- Fresh raspberries (1 cup)
- Fat free yogurt (half cup)
- Ice cubes (1 ½ cups)
- Honey (1 tsp)

Direction

Combine all the ingredients in the blender bowl and blend them with few high speed pulses. Pour them into glasses and serve this smoothie.

Mango peach and banana smoothie

Ingredients

- Frozen peach slices(1 ½ cups)
- Mango nectar (1 can about 16 ounce)
- Peach yogurt (1 cup)
- Banana (1 frozen, cut into chunks)
- Frozen yogurt (1 cup)

Direction

Combine all the ingredients in the blender bowl and mix them well. Give it few high speed pulses and pour them into glasses.

Tropical Smoothie with kale smoothie

Ingredients

- Kale (1 cup, chopped)
- Banana (1, cut into chunks)
- Almond milk (1 cup, or required accordingly)
- Frozen pineapple chunks (1 ½ cups)

Direction

Combine all the four ingredients in the blender and blend them well until completely smooth. Pour into glasses and serve them well.

Pineapple and banana smoothie

Ingredients

- Ice cubes (4)
- Fresh Pineapple (1/4 peeled, cored and cubed)
- Banana (1 large, cut into chunks)
- Pineapple (1 cup) or apple juice

Direction

Combine all the four ingredients to the blender and blend them well. Blend for 30 sec to 1 min until completely smooth. Pour into glasses and serve well.

Green power and Mojito Smoothie

Ingredients

- Banana (1 large, cut into chunks)
- Orange (1, peeled and segmented)
- Pineapple (1 can about 7 ounce)
- Water (half cup)
- Fresh mint leaves (10 or more for taste)
- Ice cubes (3 cups)
- Spinach leaves (2 cups)
- Lemon juice (1)
- Lime juice (1)

Direction

Combine all the ingredients to the blender along with ice cubes. Blend them and pour into the glasses and serve it well. Enjoy the healthy smoothie.

Super Smooth

Ingredients

- Blueberries (1 cup, frozen)
- Water (half cup)

- Yogurt (half cup)
- Ice cubes (half cup, crushed)
- Sliced banana (half cup)
- Cucumber (half cup, sliced)

Direction

Combine all the ingredients to the blender and blend it well. Pour it into glasses and serve it well.

Island Smoothie

Ingredients

- Ice cubes (1 cup)
- Ginger ale (half cup)
- Coconut milk (3 tbsp)
- Pineapple juice (2 cups)
- White sugar (1 tbsp)

Direction

Combine all the ingredients to the blender or mixer. Blend with few high speed pulses and pour it into glasses.

Hailey's Smoothie

Ingredients

- Plain yogurt (1 cup)\
- Kiwi (3, peeled and chopped)
- Blueberries (1 cup)
- Ice cubes (1 ½ cups, crushed)
- Bananas (2 frozen, peeled and chopped)
- Honey (3 tbsp)

Direction

Combine all the ingredients and give it few high speed pulses until completely smooth. Pour into glasses and serve.

Avocado Smoothie

Ingredients

- Honey (3 tbsp)
- Avocado (1 ripe, halved and pitted)
- Milk (1 cup)
- Yogurt (half cup)

- Ice cubes (8)

Direction

Combine all the ingredients and blend them well. Pour into glasses and serve this yummy recipe.

Yummy Smoothie

Ingredients

- Milk (1/4 cup)
- Frozen strawberries (half cup)
- Ice cubes (half cup)
- Frozen peach slices (half cup)

Direction

Combine all the ingredients to the blender jar and blend it well. Give it few high speed pulses and pour them into glasses.

Peach Smoothie

Ingredients

- Peaches (1 can about 15 sliced, drained)
- Orange juice (1/4 cup)
- Ice cream (4 scoops)
- Soy milk (2 cups)

Direction

Combine all the ingredients to the blender jar and blend them well. Give it few high speed pulses until completely blend. Pour into glasses and serve.

B and L Strawberry Smooth

Ingredients

- Strawberries (8, hulled)
- Ice cubes (6 cubes, crushed)
- Skim milk (half cup)
- Plain yogurt (half cup)
- White sugar (3 tbsp)

Direction

Combine all the ingredients to the blender bowl and blend until completely smooth. Mix it well and pour into glasses and serve it well.

Mango peach Smoothie

Ingredients

- Soy milk (half cup)
- Peach (1 slice)
- Mango (1, peeled and diced)
- Orange juice (half cup)

Direction

Combine all the ingredients to the blender bowl and blend it completely with high speed pulses until completely smooth. Pour into glasses and serve.

Coconut Berry Green Smoothies

Ingredients

- Coconut water (1 cup)
- Blueberries (1 cup)

- Goji berries (¼ cup)
- 2 handful greens

Direction

Add greens and coconut water to blender jar and blend them completely. Add the rest of ingredients and blend again. Pour into glasses and serve delicious smoothie.

Banana Mango Green Smoothie

Ingredients

- 1 frozen banana, peeled
- Water (2 cups)
- Spirulina (2 tsp)
- Mango chunks (½ cup), frozen
- 2 handful greens

Direction

Add water and greens to the blender jar and blend it completely. Add the rest of ingredients and blend them again. When completely done, pour into glasses and serve.

Orange Avocado Green Smoothie

Ingredients

- 3 oranges, peeled
- Spirulina powder (2 tbsp)
- Ice cubes (½ cup)
- Water (1 cup)
- 2 handful greens
- ½ avocado, peeled and pitted

Direction

Add greens and water to the blender jar and blend completely. Add the rest of ingredients and blend them again. Pour into glasses and serve.

Banana Nut Green Smoothie

Ingredients

- Almond milk (1 cup)
- 2 frozen bananas, peeled
- 2 handful greens
- Ground flax seeds (2 tbsp)
- Cacao (2 tbsp)

Direction

Add greens and almond milk together to the blender jar. Blend them well and add the rest of ingredients to the blender jar and blend them completely. Pour into glasses and serve.

Cherry Wheatgrass Green Smoothie

Ingredients

- Frozen cherries (1 cup)
- Water (1 cup)
- Fresh beet juice (½ cup)
- 2 handful greens
- 4 large dates, pitted
- Chia seeds (¼ cup)
- Fresh wheatgrass juice (½ cup)

Direction

Add greens and water to the blender jar and blend well. Add the rest of ingredients and blend well. When completely done, pour into glasses and serve.

Banana Rice Protein Green Smoothie

Ingredients

- Ice cubes (2 cups)
- Protein powder (½ cup), plant based
- Cashews (1/3 cup)
- Celery (2 cups), chopped
- Spirulina (1 tbsp)
- 3 peeled bananas

Direction

Combine all the ingredients to the blender jar and blend it well. Pour into glasses and serve.

Berry Protein Green Smoothie

Ingredients

- Cacao powder (½ cup)
- Frozen raspberries (1 ½ cups)
- 2 handful greens
- Plant based protein powder (½ cup)
- Frozen blueberries (¼ cup)
- Water (2 cups)

- Almond butter (¼ cup)

Direction

Add greens and water to the blender jar and blend it well. When get the desired thickness, add the rest of ingredients and blend again. Pour into glasses and serve.

Cucumber Strawberry Green Smoothie

Ingredients

- Ground flaxseeds (2 tbsp)
- 1 cucumber
- 2 handful greens
- Frozen strawberries (1 cup)
- Water (1 cup)
- 4 dried figs

Direction

Add all the ingredients to the blender jar and blend them well. When completely done, pour into glasses and serve.

Cranberry Green Smoothie

Ingredients

- Ground chia seeds (1 tbsp)
- Ice cubes (½ cup)
- 2 handful greens
- Blackberries (½ cup)
- Blueberries (½ cup)

Direction

Add greens and ice cubes to the blender jar and blend completely. When completely done, add the rest of ingredients and blend again. Pour into glasses and serve.

Carrot Apple Green Smoothie

Ingredients

- Ice cubes (1 cup)
- 1 small beet, diced and peeled

- Water (1 cup)
- 2 stalks celery
- 2 handful greens
- 1 apple
- ½ lemon, peeled and sectioned
- 2 carrots

Direction

Add water and greens to the blender jar and blend it completely. When get the desired thickness, add the rest of ingredients and blend again. When completely done, pour into glasses and serve.

Green Berry Smoothie

Ingredients

- Water (½ cup)
- 2 handful greens
- 1 Frozen banana, peeled
- Mix berries (2 cups)
- Green tea (½ cup)

Direction

Add water and greens to the blender jar and blend.

When get the desired thickness, add the rest of ingredients and blend again until smoothie is ready. Pour into glasses and serve.

Apple Pear Green Smoothie

Ingredients

- Fresh lemon juice (2 tbsp)
- 1 seed pear
- Water (½ cup)
- 2 handful greens
- 1 large apple
- 2 stalks celery, chopped
- 1 frozen banana, peeled

Direction

Add water and greens together to the blender jar and blend it completely. Add the rest of ingredients and blend again. Blend until smoothie is ready. Pour into glasses and serve.

Banana Pear Green Smoothie

Ingredients

- 2 pears
- 2 handful greens
- Almond (1/3 cup)
- 1 Frozen banana, peeled
- Water (1 ½ cups)

Direction

Add all the ingredients to the blender and blend them completely. Pour into glasses and serve delicious green smoothie.

Orange Spinach Green Smoothie

Ingredients

- Apple (1 tbsp)

- Stevia (1 packet)
- 1 orange, peeled and seeded
- Baby spinach (2 cups)

Direction

Add water and greens to the blender jar and blend them completely. Add the rest of ingredients and blend them well. When ready, pour into glasses and serve.

Papaya Lemon Green Smoothie

Ingredients
- 1 lemon
- Papaya chunks (1 cup)
- 1 frozen banana, peeled
- 1 handful parsley
- Water (2 cups)

Direction

Add all the ingredients to the food processor and blend them well. When smoothie is ready, pour into glasses and serve this delicious, easy to make green smoothie.

Mango Banana Green Smoothie

Ingredients

- Coconut water (1 cup)
- Mango chunks (1 ½ cup), frozen
- 1 peeled banana
- 2 handful greens

Direction

Add all the ingredients to the blender and blend until completely done. Pour into glasses and serve.

Banana Nut Green Smoothie

Ingredients

- Chia seeds (2 tbsp)
- 2 handful greens
- 3 peeled banana
- Almond milk (1 ½ cups)

Direction

Combine all the ingredients and add them to the blender. Blend them completely and pour them into glasses and serve.

Watermelon Ginger Green Smoothie

Ingredients

- Chia seeds (2 tbsp)
- Watermelon chunks (4 cups)
- Fresh peeled ginger (1 inch)
- 2 handful greens
- Ice cube (½ cup)

Direction

Combine greens and water and add them to the blender. Mix them, when they are consistent, add the rest of ingredients and blend them again. When smoothie is ready, pour into glasses and serve.

Berry Coconut Green Smoothie

Ingredients

- Frozen blueberries (½ cup)
- Coconut water (1 ½ cups)
- Raspberries (½ cup), frozen
- 2 handful greens

Direction

Combine greens and water in a bowl and add them to the blender. Blend when they are completely mix and consistent. Afterward add the rest of ingredients and blend them again. When smoothie is ready, pour them into glasses and serve.

Conclusion

So there you have it! Incorporating these deliciously health-boosting smoothies will not only give your body a fabulous boost of vitamins and nutrients, they will also help boost various functions and aspects of your body! Whether you're looking to lose weight, improve various health conditions, boost your skin's appearance, or add some excitement to the bedroom, smoothies are an amazingly delicious and effective solution to all of these things! Cheers to good health and improved quality in all aspects of life! Drink up.

www.ingramcontent.com/pod-product-compliance
Lightning Source LLC
Chambersburg PA
CBHW071445070526
44578CB00001B/209